D1177957

PHOTOGRADE

A PHOTOGRAPHIC GRADING ENCYCLOPEDIA FOR UNITED STATES COINS

A Guide to Evaluating the Features Which Determine
the Price of Rare Coins

By: James F. Ruddy

Member International Association of Professional Numismatists
Life Member American Numismatic Association
Member American Numismatic Society

All photographs by the author.

Published under license from
Bowers and Merena Galleries, Inc. by
Zyrus Press Inc., P.O. Box 17810, Irvine, CA 92623
ISBN: 0-9742371-5-9

Printed in the United States of America

TO JIM RUDDY

Q. David Bowers, author of the expanded text in the present volume, respectfully dedicates this book to his close friend and business associate for many years, *Jim Ruddy*, creator of *Photograde*, whose thousands of hours of tireless effort produced the photographs and grading descriptions employed in the volume. During his numismatic career, which commenced in 1953 and continued until his retirement in 1977, Jim Ruddy was a collector's collector, a dealer's dealer. His wisdom, counsel, sense of fairness, and business ethics set a high professional standard.

JOIN TODAY!

American Numismatic Association
818 N. Cascade Avenue
Colorado Springs, CO 80903
Tel: 800-514-2646 / Fax: 719-634-4085
w w w . m o n e y . o r g

*The world's largest non profit numismatic organization invites
your membership application today.*

Table of Contents

Table of Contents, Continued

Acknowledgments

Photograde was first published in 1970. This new edition has a considerably revised and expanded text by Q. David Bowers. Grateful appreciation is extended to James F. Ruddy, whose original photographs and grading descriptions form the corpus of the grading section of the present work, and for his many valuable suggestions and comments since the time the first edition was published.

Appreciation is also extended to the countless individuals who over a long span of years have made suggestions leading to the improvement of the book.

Chapter 1

Coin Grading Essentials

At the outset it is important to note that the grade of a coin is only one element of a coin's value. Auction records, dealers' lists, and other sources confirm that not all coins within a given grade have equal value.

For example, a Mint State-65 coin of given issue can be worth $1,000, or $600, or $1,500 depending upon other aspects such as sharpness of striking, centering, planchet quality, toning or absence thereof, and overall aesthetic appeal. In a brochure, the American Numismatic Association Grading Service noted that depending upon certain characteristics, certain MS-65 coins could have the value of MS-63 coins, or, conversely, certain attractive AU-55 coins could be worth as much as MS-63 coins.

This is a very important point, and one which should not be overlooked, for if you buy a coin based only upon its "technical grade," you may think you are buying a bargain, but if it is not sharply struck, or if it has an unsatisfactory planchet, or if it is poorly centered, or if it lacks that undefinable quality known as aesthetic appeal, it may not excite enthusiasm on the part of a buyer when time comes to sell it.

Coin Descriptions

In describing coins, any significant marks, defects, or problems should be noted separately if they are not normal for the grade. In a coin in About Good, Good, Very Good, or some lesser grade, some nicks, small marks, and other evidences of handling, in addition to wear, are normal and need not be mentioned unless they are particularly obvious or disfiguring. However, on a high-grade Uncirculated or Proof coin, a cut, edge bump, mark, or other significant impairment should be specifically described. In 1949, Dr. William H. Sheldon in *Early American Cents* specifically stated: "It is probably best to grade the coin as if *without* the injury, then to list or describe the injury separately. This procedure is usually followed by cataloguers when the coin is of any importance or has any particular value."

Not everyone subscribes to this philosophy. In the opinion of the writer, the more information given to a prospective buyer, the better the prospective buyer will be able to understand the coin offered. Thus, a description such as: "Proof-65, with brilliant fields, light iridescent toning around the border, and with a small planchet defect on the rim opposite the first numeral of the date" is more satisfactory and gives a better "word picture" of the coin than does simply "Proof-65." Also, the description calls attention to a planchet defect which should be mentioned.

Some suggest that rather than mention the planchet defect, for example, the coin should be assigned a lower grade, with nothing else stated. Thus, for the preceding coin a description such as "Proof-63" would be appropriate. Upon viewing a coin, the buyer will then note that it is a higher grade coin, a Proof-65, but with a planchet defect, and may calculate that with the defect the coin has the *value* of a Proof-63 coin. If so, all will be well in the transaction. However, for our money, the more specific a description can be, the better.

General Grading Definitions

The following definitions are general and are given for basic information only. For specific coins, refer to each type illustrated and described in the grading section of the book.

The adjectival grade is given, followed by the numerical abbreviation. The numbers are adapted from the Sheldon Scale first proposed in 1949, with additions, deletions, and modifications, and are cross-referenced to the ANA grading system (effective with the third edition of the *Official ANA Grading Standards for United States Coins* published in 1987).

POOR-1. Never abbreviated. Equal to Dr. Sheldon's Basal State-1. A coin which is worn so smooth it is barely identifiable as to type. Most of the lettering, numerals, etc. are worn away. Coins in this condition are rarely collected.

FAIR-2. Never abbreviated. A coin which is well worn and which is identifiable as to type, with a few scattered letters or perhaps one or two date numerals visible, but not necessarily identifiable by date or mintmark variety. Coins in this grade are seldom collected.

ABOUT GOOD; AG-3. This grade represents a well worn coin which can still be identified, but barely, as to date and mint. This is the lowest grade individually described in the Photograde text or in the book *Official ANA Grading Standards for United States Coins.*

GOOD; G-4. This grade usually indicates an overall clean appearing coin with all major lettering visible and with basic features outlined, except for coins dated in the 1790s and early 1800s, which may have certain portions of the inscriptions missing, but with the date numerals distinct. On certain issues, such as Indian cents and Liberty Seated coins, the word LIBERTY will not be visible. Dr. Sheldon proposed G-5 and G-6, but these intermediate grades are seldom used.

VERY GOOD; VG-8. This is probably one of the easiest grades to describe. In many cases the word LIBERTY on the headband or shield can be used to determine the grade. When it is stated that a total of any three letters of LIBERTY verify this grade, it is taking into consideration the many diverse designs used on all our coins. In some cases three full letters may be visible, in other cases two full and two partial letters or even one full and four partial letters will show. Of course, it is important that all other features of both the obverse and reverse verify this grade. Dr. Sheldon also lists VG-9 and VG-10, intermediate grades seldom used today.

FINE; F-12. This condition represents what is probably the most widely collected circulated grade. All the major design features are usually visible. The word LIBERTY is complete (except on 20-cent pieces and Liberty Seated silver dollars). Dr. Sheldon proposed F-15 as well, and this designation is sometimes seen, representing a coin slightly nicer than F-12.

VERY FINE; VF-20 and VF-30. On a VF-20 example some of the more intricate designs will be noticeable. A careful eye is needed to distinguish the differences between Very Fine-20 and 30 and the next highest grade, Extremely Fine-40. Very Fine-30 represents a particularly nice VF example. The American Numismatic Association designates VF-20 coins as Typical Very Fine and VF-30 coins as Choice Very Fine. Sometimes a further intermediate grade, VF-35, is used.

EXTREMELY FINE; EF-40 and EF-45. Practically all details will be clearly visible. An EF-45 example will often show traces of mint lustre, particularly in protected areas among letters. The American Numismatic Association designates EF-40 as Typical Extremely Fine and EF-45 as Choice Extremely Fine.

ABOUT UNCIRCULATED; AU-50, AU-55, and AU-58. Sometimes designated as Almost Uncirculated. A coin which has seen just a slight amount of circulation but which usually possesses much original mint lustre in the field, as well as in protected areas. The American Numismatic Association designates AU-50 as Typical About Uncirculated, AU-55 as Choice About Uncirculated, and AU-58 as Very Choice About Uncirculated. In practice, such distinctions are difficult to define or use. An AU-58 coin is one which years ago would have been called "borderline Uncirculated," a piece which possesses nearly the full characteristics of an Uncirculated coin, except where some slight friction is on the higher points.

UNCIRCULATED; MS-60, MS-61, MS-62, MS-63, MS-64, MS-65, MS-66, MS-67, MS-68, MS-69, MS-70. An Uncirculated or Mint State coin is one which has never seen circulation. However, due to the minting process, bagging, and other handling at the mint and at various banks, the coin can show nicks, marks, scuffs and abrasions. A coin with numerous such marks is at the low end of the scale, MS-60, whereas an absolutely perfect coin is at the high end, MS-70. Dr. Sheldon recognized three ranges when he proposed his numerical system in 1949: MS-60, MS-65, and MS-70, an MS-65 coin being an intermediate piece with just a few marks. In 1986, the ANA Board of Governors adopted several "new" or intermediate grades for Uncirculated coins. Thus, listings such as MS-61, MS-62, etc. represent intermediate grades.

MS-60. This grade, at the low end of the Uncirculated scale, represents a coin which has never been in the channels of circulation, but which has numerous bagmarks and other evidences of coin-to-coin contact. However, traces of sliding wear, friction in the fields, and heavy rubbing are not seen. On a large and heavy coin, such as a silver dollar, the bagmarks may be quite heavy and extensive.

MS-65. An Uncirculated coin which possesses only a few scattered bagmarks or hairlines, none of which is disfiguring. By current definition, such a coin is one of excellent quality with an overall pleasing aspect.

MS-70. An absolutely perfect Uncirculated coin. Under magnification with a hand glass, no contact or other marks are to be seen. In general, such perfection is only found among modern coins specifically issued at a premium price for collectors.

MS-61, MS-62, MS-63, MS-64, MS-66, MS-67, MS-68, and MS-69 represent intermediate grades which have not been defined with precision. What may be one person's MS-61 may be another's MS-60 or MS-62. In an effort to establish benchmarks for intermediate grades, the American Numismatic Association, the Numismatic Guaranty Corporation, PCGS, and others have been building reference coin sets, but thus far no information has appeared in print which will permit grading on a consistent basis by an outsider. As we go to press, it is the case that certain coins submitted to grading services at different times are in many instances assigned different grades. Although such numbers as MS-61, MS-62, etc. suggest a fine degree of precision, to date such precision has not been achieved on a consistent basis. If the various intermediate grades between MS-60 and MS-70 are ever codified with precision, so that a knowledgeable numismatist using such descriptions can accurately grade coins, then such descriptions will be included in future *Photograde* editions.

PROOF; Proof-60 through Proof-70. A Proof coin should have no wear, friction, or rubbing of any kind unless it is impaired and so noted. Occasionally the mirror-like surfaces will show minor hairlines, usually caused by rubbing of a cloth during a cleaning operation. On a Proof-60 coin, hairlines, scuffs, and other marks will be in abundance, whereas a Proof-70 coin represents perfection. The middle grade, Proof-65, represents a piece with only a few scattered very light hairlines, a few contact marks, and no major impairments. Other Proof grades are intermediate variations of these basic definitions.

Matte Proof copper or nickel coins, made in the Lincoln cent series from 1909 to 1916 and the Buffalo nickel series from 1913 to 1916, must have an absolutely square rim, be well centered, have a mirror-like edge, and a grainy, matte surface (and not have mint frost or cartwheel lustre). There are many deceptive Uncirculated coins which closely resemble Proofs, so the identification of a Matte Proof is best done with the assistance of a professional until you become acquainted with the distinctive appearance of such issues. Sandblast Proof, Roman Finish Proof, and Satin Proof coins were made of certain issues in the Pratt Indian Head gold quarter eagle and half eagle series and the Saint-Gaudens $10 and $20 series and likewise should be verified by an expert, as certain Uncirculated coins resemble these closely.

Other Grading Considerations

Intermediate Grades. Coins with grades falling between the categories listed can be assigned accepted intermediate grades such as VF-30, EF-45, etc.

Split Grades. Split grades are often advertised in order to more accurately describe a coin. A coin described as Good to Very Good (G-4 – VG-8) may show evidence of a letter or two of "LIBERTY" (if that is the diagnostic grading feature) but not the total of three letters necessary to call it Very Good. If a coin has a Fine obverse but only a Very Good reverse (when obverse and reverse grades differ, it is customary to note this by a slash mark [/] as in F-12/VG-8). This is not illogical. Sometimes a coin will be struck with a high protective rim on the obverse and a low rim on the reverse; a situation which causes the reverse to wear more quickly. Other examples exist. The more valuable a coin is, the more reason there is to use split grades. If a coin catalogues for $20 Good and $35 Very Good, then using the split grade of G-4/VG-8 may make a difference of several dollars in value. This is an important consideration for both the buyer and seller.

In the numerical grading system, split grades are indicated by numbers such as VG-8/F-12 or, in the instance in which the prefix letters are the same, MS-60/63.

The first illustration describes a coin with a VG-8 obverse and a Fine-12 reverse, while the second describes a coin with a Mint State-60 obverse and Mint State-63 reverse.

Chapter 2

Grading Practices and Formulas

Historical Grading

In the early 19th century, coins were described in auction catalogues and periodicals by use of simple adjectival terms, such as Poor, Good, Fine, Uncirculated, and Proof. Sometimes the terms were slightly confusing, such as the notation in an 1866 issue of the *American Journal of Numismatics* referring to a "very fine proof" cent of 1844. Decades later, it became common practice to capitalize adjectives specifically intended for grading, so a later description of the same piece might have been printed as "very fine Proof," leading the reader to believe that the coin was a Proof, but a "nice" example (in other words, very fine did not pertain to a specific grade in this instance). However, Very Fine indeed was a grade on its own then, and the same account notes a 1787 Nova Eborac copper coin described as "very fine." Confusion reigned!

Without an explanation of what various terms such as Good, Fine, Very Fine, Extremely Fine, Uncirculated, and Proof meant, there were often heated discussions concerning the status of a given coin. What one dealer called Uncirculated, a competitor might view as just Fine, or worse! John W. Haseltine, a leading dealer of the time, in September 1873 attended the sale of the J.M. MacAllister Collection catalogued by a New York competitor, William H. Strobridge, and subsequently wrote to a client, John Tinkham, that "everything in it was miserable, nothing near the description."

No refinements or codifications were made in grading, and without further explanations or a common reference source, dealers applied adjectives based upon their own personal experience.

In 1934 Wayte Raymond, a New York dealer and numismatic scholar, launched the *Standard Catalogue of United States Coins*, which went through nearly 20 editions by the time Raymond died in the late 1950s. Grading was basic, with such terms as Good, Fine, Very Fine, Uncirculated, and Proof employed. Various editions incorporated a scale of conditions. For example, in the 1954 edition the following grades were listed and explained:

Proof— specially struck coins generally with a mirror-like surface sold to collectors at the United States Mint.

Uncirculated— A new coin showing no evidence of circulation, although not necessarily brilliant.

Extremely Fine— A new coin displaying only the lightest rubbing or friction on the highest parts.

Very Fine— Showing only light evidence of circulation.

Fine— Showing slight signs of wear but still an attractive piece.

Very Good— showing more or less wear but lettering clear and plain.

Good— Showing greater wear with higher parts of a design partially gone.

Fair— Considerably worn and type does not all show.

At the time, grades were approximate, and without a specific definition, what one dealer called Fine another might call Very Fine or Very Good.

In 1946 the Whitman Publishing Company issued the first annual edition of *A Guide Book of United States Coins*, which listed values of various colonial and regular issues. Basic adjectival grades were employed, such as Good, Fine, Uncirculated, and Proof, with no definitions or explanations given.

Later editions of the *Guide Book* gave a basic scale title of "Condition of Coins." The following is from the 1954-1955 edition:

Coins listed in this volume are priced in the conditions usually available from dealers. Columns are headed with one or more of the following condition classifications:

Good. A coin that has had considerable wear. Every important part of the design is still plain.

V. Good or Very Good. Better condition than Good, but not quite Fine.

Fine. Show circulation but only worn on high points. Design and details are sharp.

V. Fine or Very Fine. Less wear from circulation and sharper than above grade. Extra Fine, Extremely Fine and About Uncirculated are terms frequently used to describe the degree of wear between Very Fine and Uncirculated.

UNC. or Uncirculated. No wear. There are various terms used to describe the state of preservation of an Uncirculated coin such as dull, brown, red, bright, brilliant and Gem.

PF or Proof. Specially struck coins, with a mirror-like surface, for collectors. Also sandblast or matte Proof.

In the meantime, various articles and essays on the subject of grading had appeared and were continuing to appear in various numismatic periodicals, including *The Numismatist* and *The Numismatic Scrapbook Magazine*. Edward Catich and Loyd Gettys collaborated on a series of articles explaining points of wear on commemorative and other coins. Another author suggested that the grades of coins could be determined by weighing them, and still others advanced further ideas.

The Brown and Dunn Book

In 1958, Martin R. Brown and John W. Dunn released the first of several editions of *A Guide to the Grading of United States Coins*. For the first time in numismatic history, a single widely distributed volume was devoted expressly to the delineation of grades of various United States coins from half cents to double eagles. Major types were illustrated by pen and ink drawings.

Adjectival descriptions were given for various classifications. For example, half cents of the 1794-1797 style were sketched and described in Fair, About Good, Good, Very Good, Fine, Very Fine, Extremely Fine and About Uncirculated classifications. The same basic grades, with some variations, were extended through the rest of the book. Uncirculated coins were not delineated, except in a general way in the introduction, which stated:

> Even in Uncirculated coins there are grades. A coin may be strictly Uncirculated and not yet exactly a perfect coin. This may be due to a poor job at the mint or bad handling by the mint and distribution agencies, causing rim nicks, scratches, scuffed places. Larger coins—dollars, half dollars, and even quarter dollars—because of their weight tend to be scratched and nicked as they are handled and shipped in bags.
>
> For Uncirculated coins, the more choice specimens—free from rim nicks, scratches, scuffed places and perfectly struck—are more desirable. They are described by various trade names: Choice, A-l, Select, Gem.

The Brown and Dunn book filled a niche, and the volume met a ready market. In 1962, publication of the work was taken over by the Whitman Publishing Company, which produced several later editions. At the time, certain information from the Brown and Dunn work was incorporated into current editions of *A Guide Book of United States Coins* and *A Handbook of United States Coins*.

Photograde by James F. Ruddy

In 1970 the first edition of *Photograde*, the work you are reading now, appeared on the numismatic scene. The introduction to the volume gave the reason for the production of *Photograde* and some philosophy:

> People have been collecting coins for over 2,000 years— making numismatics one of the oldest hobbies in the world. Before the 20th century many collectors graded their coins as being either "new" or "used." Rarely did the price of a coin dictate that a finer distinction in grading be made. Most often, coins could be purchased for a small premium over their face value.

The story today is much different. Since the numismatic boom began in the 1950s there has been an ever-increasing demand for rare coins. The supply remains constant as the mintage of a given issue cannot be changed. The natural result is a rise in values. This happened in the 1950s. And when it did, it became increasingly more important to grade coins carefully. The difference between Good and Fine might have meant $1 to $2 in the price of a particular coin in 1950. By the 1970s this same grading difference might have meant $50 to $100.

The numismatic hobby of the 1950s fully realized the need to provide pricing and grading guides that would keep the collector well informed. *The Guide Book*, the standard pricing reference, was expanded and improved. A weekly newspaper, *Coin World*, appeared in 1960 and offered a regular section which featured coin values. *Numismatic News*, another weekly paper, offered its "Tele-Quotes" guide to values.

However, in the field of coin grading much less progress has been made. In 1958 Messrs. Brown and Dunn pioneered the standardization of grading with a book which used line drawings to illustrate wear on a coin. Attempts were made by others to create grading reference books by using photographs of actual coins. Unfortunately, the photographic reproduction and, in a few cases, the grading information was inadequate to warrant the acceptance of these works as a standard.

Today we are faced with the paradox of excellent progress in pricing information, but we have little that is new in grading guidelines since 1958. Pricing and grading are equally important as the value of a coin depends not only on its date and mintmark but on its grade as well. For example, if a coin catalogues $100 Fine, $200 Very Fine, and $300 Extremely Fine, not knowing whether a coin is Very Fine can be expensive. If you are offered a purported Very Fine for $200, and it is really only Fine, you've lost $100. On the other hand, if it is really Extremely Fine, you've made a windfall profit of

$100! Check the prices in Fine, Very Fine, and Extremely Fine of a cent of 1793 or 1877, a 1916-D dime, or any one of hundreds of other examples, and you will see well the need for all collectors and dealers to have an accurate modern pictorial grading guide!

In 1968, after carefully considering the problems involved, I decided to write a book that would fill this need. I knew that four important factors were necessary to produce a successful photographic grading guide:

First was the access to hundreds of thousands of dollars worth of coins needed for photography. For two years I systematically took pictures of every coin that came through my hands which best represented the average grade for its type. Additional coins and other help were provided by Jan Bronson, Jerry Cohen, Joe Flynn, Jr., and Abner Kreisberg. Q. David Bowers, my long-time business associate, provided other valuable assistance.

Next came research. Fortunately I have had nearly two decades of professional coin dealing experience to draw from. In this time I have graded tens of millions of dollars worth of coins. My schooling and professional training was originally in scientific research. This background taught me to be precise and methodical on very minute details — important factors when formalizing a universal grading system.

Next came photography — by far the most formidable feature to master. The main problem was the extremes involved; the wide range in detail from About Good to About Uncirculated; the size differential from silver three cent pieces to silver dollars; the variations from a dark porous copper surface to a brilliant silver or gold one. Again, I was fortunate to have a background which was of immeasurable help. Before coins became my career I worked with the Physics Research Laboratory of Ansco Film Company. There I performed research on all aspects of photographic resolution. Even with this experience it took weeks of research to match the right camera, film, and light meter to produce the desired results. The camera I chose was an

Exackta with a 50 mm. fl.9 lens and a through-the-lens metering system. The film was picked not to give "pretty" or "artistic-appearing" pictures, but to give extremely high resolution, high contrast, and fine grain features. Lighting was of paramount importance. Hundreds of test exposures utilizing dozens of various lighting conditions were tried before the first coin picture was taken. Experiments in film processing, background color, and the size of the printed coin picture were also necessary. I took over 5,000 photographs to achieve the desired results. In many instances a single exposure produced the perfect representation of a certain grade of the type. In other cases it took as many as 20 pictures to produce a single satisfactory one. There are over 1,000 different pictures in this book— many more than in any other grading guide.

Photograde was an instant success, and by January 1988, 16 printings had occurred, comprising the best part of a half million copies, making the book far and away the best-selling grading guide ever published.

In 1972 *Photograde* received the honor of being designated as an official grading guide by the American Numismatic Association, a distinction that was noted on the cover of subsequent printings. After 1977, when the American Numismatic Association devised a numerical grading system (more about this later) *Photograde* incorporated a cross-reference to the numbers.

Numerical Grading

Numerical grading as practiced today had its beginnings in the Sheldon Scale, devised by Dr. William H. Sheldon and published in his book, *Early American Cents* (later retitled to *Penny Whimsy*) in 1949 as part of a formula for determining the market value of United States large cents of the dates 1793-1814. Being of a scientific turn of mind, Dr. Sheldon endeavored to reduce grading to quantitative terms. Working backward, he sought to devise a series of numbers, which when applied to coins, would act as a multiplier to determine the current market price.

Each variety of cent from 1793 to 1814 was assigned a Basal Value, a base price which varied from variety to variety depending upon the desirability of the coin as a design type, the rarity of the issue, or some other consideration. Thus, a certain variety of 1802 cent, a relatively common date, might have been given a Basal Value of $1, whereas a certain 1793, a scarce date, would merit a Basal Value of $5.

Prior to the publication of Dr. Sheldon's work, grading was strictly adjectival. Such descriptions as Good, Very Good, Fine, Very Fine, Extremely Fine, About Uncirculated, Uncirculated, and Proof sufficed for transactions. Sometimes an intermediate grade would be used, such as Very Fine to Extremely Fine.

Dr. Sheldon assigned numbers to these different descriptions. More about this later, but for purposes of the present introduction, representative numbers included Good-4, Very Fine-30, About Uncirculated-50, and Mint State (Sheldon's term for Uncirculated, now widely adopted) -60, abbreviated as MS-60. A particularly attractive Uncirculated coin with few defects was described as MS-65, and a perfect Uncirculated coin, with full original color, as MS-70.

According to Dr. Sheldon's formula, an 1802 cent with a Basal Value of $1, and in VF-30 grade, was worth $1 x 30, or $30. A 1793 cent with a Basal Value of $5, and in VF-30 grade, was worth $5 x 30, or $150. So far so good.

An 1802 cent with a Basal Value of $1, if in MS-60 grade, was worth $1 x 60, or $60, while a 1793 cent, if in Uncirculated grade, was worth $5 x 60, or $300. In 1949, when the formula was introduced, it was the case in many instances that an MS-60 coin was worth just twice the price of VF-30 example, for collectors as a group had not become as condition conscious as they were to be in later years. This situation continued in the market until about 1953, when collectors realized that Uncirculated (Mint State) coins were much more desirable than worn pieces, and the differential widened greatly. Today, in 1988 as these words are being written, a VF-30 1802 cent may be worth approximately $200 according to the Sheldon formula, and an MS-60 coin, with a grading number twice that of 30, should be worth twice as much, or $400. However, an MS-60 1802 cent is more likely to be worth $2,000 to $4,000, or 10 to 20 times more than a VF-30 coin. Clearly, the use of numerical grading as a market formula is obsolete.

If one were to assume that grading numbers are part of a market formula, then the numbers would have to be changed. If an Uncirculated 1802 cent is worth $2,000, or 10 times as much as a VF-30 coin, then the numerical value for an Uncirculated coin should be 10 times as much, or 200 instead of 20, thus Mint State-200. Of course, if in the future the taste of collectors should change again, and Uncirculated coins are not as strongly desired in relation to circulated ones, then the numbers would have to be revised downward. Or, if a fantastic demand for Uncirculated coins developed, and the price of an Uncirculated coin increased to 50 times the price of a VF-30 example, the numbers would have to be increased. Stated simply, by 1953 the Sheldon numerical scale of grading had become meaningless in relation to its original purpose.

However, for many there is safety in numbers, so to speak, and the idea of numerical grading caught on. By the 1970s, numerous dealers and collectors were applying numbers to many other areas besides United States large cents of the 1793-1814 years. Thus, Morgan silver dollars, to name one series, were often graded by numbers. As no one published a guide to what the numbers meant in relation to coins examined, interpretations of the numbers varied all over the place. What was one person's MS-65 Morgan silver dollar might have been another's MS-60, and still another's MS-70.

Gradually, numerical grading evolved and expanded. Let us trace it from its earliest steps to the present day:

The Sheldon Scale

Dr. William H. Sheldon's *Early American Cents* book presented a chart titled "A Quantitative Scale for Condition," now known simply as the Sheldon Scale. The following numbers were assigned:

Basal State-1. "Identifiable and unmutilated, but so badly worn that only a portion of the legend or inscription is legible. Enough must remain for positive identification of the variety, although for some varieties this need not necessarily include a readable date."

Fair-2. "The date and more than half the inscription and detail can be made out, although perhaps faintly."

Very Fair-3. "The date will be clear and practically all of the detail of the coin can be made out, although faint areas are to be expected, and the coin as a whole may be worn nearly smooth."

Good-4, Good-5, and Good-6. "The date together with all of the detail must be very clear. The general relief of the coin may be well worn down."

Very Good-7, Very Good-8, Very Good-10. "Everything is boldly clear, but the sharpness of the coin may be largely gone. Signs of wear arc seen uniformly over the whole coin, not merely on the high surfaces."

Fine-12, Fine-15. "All of the designs and all of the inscriptions are sharp. Wear is appreciable only on the high surfaces. If a coin is examined with a glass, the microscopic detail is gone."

Very Fine-20, Very Fine-30. "All of the detail is in sharp relief, and only the highest surfaces show wear, even when the glass is applied. The microscopic details largely intact except on the high points. These high surfaces will show a little rubbing, or flattening, even to the unaided eye."

Extremely Fine-40. "Only the slightest trace of wear, or rubbing, is to be seen on the high points."

About Uncirculated-50. "Close attention or the use of a glass should be necessary to make out that the coin is not in perfect Mint State. Typically, the AU-50 coin retains its full sharpness but is darkened or a little off color."

Mint State-60, Mint State-65, Mint State-70. "Free from any trace of wear, and the color should be that of a copper coin which has been kept with great care. The color will vary from mint red to light brown or light olive, according to the chemical content and moisture of the prevailing atmosphere in which the coin has been kept. The light brown and light olive colors indicate the first beginnings of a protective patina, or surface 'set.' When these colors are attractively blended and permanently set on a Mint State early cent, the coin is as highly prized by discerning collectors as is one of brighter color. For a Condition 60 a minor blemish, perhaps some microscopic injury, or light trace of discoloration may be tolerated. For Condition 70, the coin must be exactly as it left the dies, except for a slight mellowing of the color. Condition 60 means Mint State. Condition 70 means *perfect* Mint State."

A footnote was given as an explanation: "These descriptions are based on the supposition that no mutilations are present. Many cents have injuries, scratches, or bruises which of course detract from numismatic value and modify condition. Since there is no way of standardizing just how much a particular mutilation damages a coin, it is probably best to grade the coin as if *without* the injury, and then to list or describe the injury separately. This procedure is usually followed by cataloguers when the coin is of any importance or has any particular value. It should be noted that a number of the early varieties are always found with certain portions of the coin weak—the result of injured or bent dies. Such coins, even when in Mint State, will lack some of their detail. The cataloguer or student of coins must acquaint himself with these varieties and must learn to judge the condition of a particular cent according to the amount of actual wear after it left the dies. In this ability lies much of the skill and art of cent numismatics. The early cents present so many peculiarities and variations in the dies, as well as differences in striking and in later coloration of the copper, that even the keenest of observers could scarcely master them all in a lifetime of study."

As noted, the assignment of numbers from 1 to 70 was based upon market conditions in effect in 1949. From a scientific viewpoint, the numbers are not particularly logical. Note, for example, that the category of Very Fine begins at VF-20 grade and ends when Extremely Fine-40 is reached, or a field of 20 numbers. On the other hand, Good grade begins with Good-4 and ends when Very Good-7 is encountered, or a field of just three numbers. Uncirculated ranges from MS-60 to MS-70, or a field of 11. Why is a field of three allowed for the Good range, 11 for Uncirculated, and 20 for Very Fine? The answer is that the numbers were contrived to fit an answer known in advance, to make "scientific" an otherwise casual market structure.

The Sheldon reference book contained no grading sketches or pictures, so *experience* was necessary to apply the Sheldon Scale. Without other information, few people could look at a given example and realize that a coin which is described as having "all the details and sharp relief, and only the high surfaces show wear, even when the glass is applied; the microscopic detail is largely intact except on the high points, these high surfaces will show a little rubbing, or flattening, even to the unaided eye," is VF-20 or VF-30 (no distinction is made between the two Very Fine categories) and is a vastly better coin than one described as: "everything is boldly clear, but the sharpness of the coin may be largely gone. Signs of wear are seen uniformly over the whole coin, not merely on the high surfaces," the description applied to Very Good-7 through Very Good-10.

Restating the preceding, besides owning a copy of Dr. Sheldon's work, it was necessary to have a knowledge of large cent grading, or to have access to previously graded specimens, for Dr. Sheldon's numbers and descriptions were not sufficient on their own to permit anyone to grade coins accurately, except for the very lowest Basal State or the very highest MS-70 categories. This fact has been largely overlooked by many since that time, who have imparted a Gospel-like quality to Dr. Sheldon's grading criteria, viewing them as pronouncements from on high. However, a close study of them, as has just been done, will reveal mathematical inconsistencies and a notable lack of precise information.

It is further important to realize that Dr. Sheldon specifically stated that injuries, scratches, bruises, and other marks should be listed separately. In recent times this also has been forgotten, and there has been a prevailing philosophy, quite illogical, that all VF-20, or all MS-65, or all AU-50 coins are the same so far as desirability and value are concerned. In practice, it can be the case that one MS-60 coin may be worth, say, $1,000, another technically graded MS-60 coin can have a market value of $600, and still another may have surfaces so pleasing that it is worth $2,000.

The ANA Grading System

In the 1970s, grading became a particularly popular topic of discussion. *Photograde* had codified grades of coins from About Good to About Uncirculated, but it was not possible to take photographs of Uncirculated pieces to show significant differences in the Uncirculated grade (nor is it possible to take such photographs today). In the meantime, various sellers devised their own terminology for Uncirculated coins, including Choice Uncirculated, for an above average specimen, and Gem Uncirculated, for a piece which showed very few flaws. Others adopted the Sheldon Scale and used the numbers MS-60, MS-65, and MS-70. In the decade of the 1970s the grade MS-70, as applied to a silver dollar, did not necessarily mean a perfect coin. Rather, some designated it to mean one of the nicest Uncirculated coins of its type, but a coin that could have some nicks or other marks.

The American Numismatic Association decided to get into the grading game, and under the direction of Virgil Hancock, president of the organization, various investigations were instituted and committees were set up. Abe Kosoff, a veteran California dealer, was commissioned to formulate a grading system, while at conventions and other gatherings, meetings were held of dealers, collectors, and other interested individuals to discuss various grading philosophies. Stanley Apfelbaum, a New York dealer, set up several roundtables to pursue the subject.

By the late 1970s, Abe Kosoff, with the consent of the American Numismatic Association Board of Governors, had enlisted the services of Kenneth Bressett, of Whitman Publishing Company, to help with the editorial material for a projected grading guide, while Q. David Bowers was tapped to write an introduction to the book, giving basic grading information, facts about minting, and other aspects affecting the grade or value of a coin.

Illustrated with pen and ink drawings, the first edition of the book, titled *Official ANA Grading Standards of United States Coins*, appeared in 1977. The information given was not basically different from the *Photograde* text, and in an interview with a West Coast numismatic publisher, Kenneth Bressett stated that the new ANA system did not differ from that in *Photograde*.

During the course of Abe Kosoff's investigations, he solicited information from numismatists. Many disagreements took place, with some wanting to adopt the Sheldon Scale of numbers, others wishing to use simply adjectives, and still others proposing that new numbers be set up, possibly from 1 to 100 (which seemed to be more scientific than Sheldon's 1 to 70), or even 1 to 1,000. After considering the input, Messrs. Kosoff and Bressett decided to adopt the Sheldon Scale, simply because it was already familiar to a number of users. It was felt that adapting it, despite the many inconsistencies and imperfections, would be better than trying an entirely new range of numbers. In the Uncirculated category, MS-60, MS-65, and MS-70 were used to differentiate coins.

Several years later, the American Numismatic Association Board of Governors provided for two new grades, MS-63 and MS-67. By that time, in the Uncirculated category the adjectival descriptions and accompanying numbers were as follows: Typical Uncirculated (MS-60), Select Uncirculated (MS-63), Choice Uncirculated (MS-65), Gem Uncirculated (MS-67) and Perfect Uncirculated (MS-70).

The market did not follow the ANA grading standards consistently, and it was not at all unusual for one advertiser or another to add plus or minus marks after a number, or to use grades not in the ANA standards, such as MS-61, MS-62, etc. One dealer used continuous numbers from MS-60 through MS-70, 11 numbers in all, with plus and minus signs after each number, for a total of over 30 possibilities within the range. Still others stated they were using the ANA grading system, but for them Choice Uncirculated did not mean the ANA grade of MS-65 but, rather, meant a lessor grade, MS-63.

In 1986 a group of dealers banded together to form the Professional Coin Grading Service, often abbreviated as PCGS.

Using its own standards and ideas, not publicly disclosed, PCGS set up a system whereby coins were graded from MS-60 to MS-70 continuously, such as MS-60, MS-61, MS-62, MS-63, MS-64, etc. The pieces were encapsulated in sonically sealed holders, called "slabs" in popular parlance, with the hope that once graded and sealed, they would stay that way, and that the grading interpretations would not change (more about changing grading interpretations later).

In the meantime, the American Numismatic Association Grading Service, established in the late 1970s, was considered by many to be the official arbiter of coin grades. For a fee, the ANA Grading Service would examine a coin and issue a certificate illustrating it and stating a grade. However, although grades from About Good-3 to AU-55 were well defined and subject to very little controversy, in the Uncirculated category there was room for a great difference of opinion. The ANA grading book stated, for example, that an MS-65 coin could have "some marks" or "a few marks." Whether some marks or a few marks meant 10 marks, 111 marks, three marks, or 77 marks was left unstated, and thus different interpretations could be made and were. By early 1986, interpretations had tightened considerably, to the point at which the American Numismatic Association Board of Governors stated that certain coins certified as MS-65 by the ANA Grading Service a few years earlier were now MS-60 to MS-63.

Elsewhere, particularly in the pages of *The Coin Dealer Newsletter*, *Coin World*, and *Numismatic News*, many comments, articles, and editorials were printed on the subject of lack of precision in grading, and changing interpretations. Many collectors felt that, somehow, dealers "knew" back in 1980 and 1981 that coins they were selling then as MS-65 really weren't, and would be graded MS-60 by the ANA Grading Service later. The truth was that no one knew that changing interpretations would occur, and the effects of these interpretations fell evenly upon everyone — dealers, collectors, investors, museums, and anyone else owning coins. Much dissatisfaction was expressed in print by buyers who purchased MS-65 coins earlier, including many who had been certified by the ANA Grading Service as MS-65 earlier, who found that by early 1986 such coins were "officially" only MS-60 or so.

By sealing coins in holders, and by applying very strict grading, it was the hope of PCGS that a coin designated by the group as MS-65 in 1986 would stay in that grade and would be interpreted as MS-65 at a later date. Seeking a new hope, a new Messiah so to speak, collectors and dealers who formerly used the ANA Grading Service to certify their coins turned in large numbers to PCGS. By the summer of 1986, submissions of coins to the ANA Grading Service had dropped from 12,000 to 14,000 per month down to fewer than 5,000 per month. A crisis was at hand, revenue was dropping, and in response the ANA Board of Governors sought to bring back the lost business by copying PCGS and adding other grades. So, it was officially decreed that thenceforth the ANA grades would include MS-61, MS-62, MS-64, and other numbers not earlier used by the ANA. In addition, AU-58 was employed. However, by early 1988 the ANA Grading Service had not regained its cachet, revenues were considerably reduced, and the ANA furloughed a number of staff members.

In the autumn of 1987 a new company, the Numismatic Guaranty Corporation of America, was launched. By January 1988, it was grading approximately 11,000 coins per month. This service, too, used all numbers from MS-60 to MS-70.

In April 1987, the third edition of *The Official ANA Grading Standards for United States Coins* was released. The official new grades were incorporated into the existing text, many line drawings were replaced by illustrations from the ANA Grading Service files. There seem to be some major logical faults with the descriptions given to the 11 numerical grades from MS-60 to MS-70 inclusive. The reader is referred to page 17 of the third edition of the ANA grading guide for specific information, but some of the problems at least as perceived by the present writer, are as follows:

The new edition notes, for example, to be MS-67 a coin may have "three or four miniscule contact marks; one or two may be in prime focal areas," whereas for MS-68 it may have "three or four miniscule contact marks; none in prime focal areas," for MS-69 it may have "one or two miniscule contact marks, none in prime focal areas."

The problem with this is that a tiny coin with a small surface, a silver three-cent piece for example, with, say, four miniscule contact marks, with two being in prime focal areas, may be quite unsightly and may, in the professional experience of the present writer, not merit a MS-65 classification. On the other hand, the same four miniscule contact marks, if on a large Morgan dollar and on the reverse hidden among the eagle's feathers may be all but invisible even to the most trained eye, and such a coin may be virtually MS-70 (but not quite, for technical reasons).

Chapter 3

Commercial Grading Services

Although commercial grading services have existed ever since the ANA Certification Service decided to grade coins in the late 1970s, a major change occurred in 1986 when David Hall founded the Professional Coin Grading Service. The PCGS concept, later adapted by the Numismatic Guaranty Corporation, ANACS, and the Hallmark Grading Service, operates basically as follows:

Coins are sent by clients and members of the public to local dealers, known as submission centers. These dealers prepare the paperwork, and for a fee charged to the client, submit the coin to PCGS, NGC, or another service. Upon receipt the service opens the package, assigns the coin an identification number, and submits the coin to a panel of independent graders, who without knowledge of the coin's owner, come up with a consensus

The grading room at the Professional Coin Grading Service shows three numismatists independently viewing coins so as to eventually reach a consensus opinion. (Photo courtesy of P.C.G.S.)

grading opinion. Then one more grader, known as a finalizer, reviews the opinion and approves of it, or if the grader does not approve, he sends it back through channels for regrading. Coins which have had altered surfaces, are artificially toned, or show damage are not certified.

Once a grade has been established, the numerical designation is printed on a ticket which is enclosed with the coin in a rectangular plastic encasement, popularly known as a "slab". Sonically sealed, the slab protects the coin from further handling, thus ensuring that it will remain in the grade stated. The coin is then returned to the submission center, which in turn returns it to the client.

Near the end of the certification process each coin is sonically sealed in a holder. Shown here is the sealing device employed at PCGS. (Photo courtesy of P.C.G.S.)

The advent of unbiased third-party grading has been welcomed by many, particularly investors who on their own are not familiar with grading practices. In as much as the opinions are unbiased, such certified coins are very popular. However, it has been shown that the same coin, if submitted to another grading service, or if resubmitted to the same grading service, can be graded differently. Although, by and large, the grading services are quite consistent with the majority of items examined.

Various grading service slabs.

As the typical grading service fee is apt to be $20 or more, the services have been utilized primarily for coins of higher values, especially those in Mint State and Proof categories.

Chapter 4

Other Elements of a Coin's Value

Color of a Coin: An early copper coin showing original mint color is rare and typically commands a substantial premium. In recent decades, unscrupulous people have devised methods of cleaning and toning copper coins to give them an artificial but deceptive appearing "brilliant" surface. There is no way to accurately describe the varying results of this process, but the chapter on cleaning coins in the present text contains useful information. Your best protection is to deal only with a reputable professional dealer. A note of caution: "There is no Santa Claus in numismatics," Lee Hewitt, founder of *The Numismatic Scrapbook Magazine*, said for many years. If you are offered a coin at a bargain price, beware, for chances are excellent that the grade may not be right. This is not to say that overgraded coins always have bargain prices, for there are many overgraded coins offered at full market price as well. But in general, a bargain-priced coin, particularly an actively traded issue priced substantially below current values, should be checked carefully.

Marks and Defects: Scratches, edge bumps, bruises, gouges, attempted punctures, heavy contact marks, etc. detract from the value of a piece. An Extremely Fine coin with an edge bump may have the value of a lesser grade coin, such as a Very Fine piece, but there are no rules in this regard. Severe imperfections such as holes, deep cuts, test marks on the edge, etc. should be individually described and will substantially reduce a coin's value.

Brilliance Versus Toning: Except for copper coins, earlier noted, there is no clear distinction in the value between a toned coin and a brilliant one. Besides, a toned coin can often be made brilliant simply by careful dipping. In auctions of old-time collections, coins with attractive toning often sell for substantial premiums. On the other hand, coins with spots, blotches, oxidation patches, or unattractive toning often sell for less. Toning can be artificially applied (refer to the chapter on this subject in the present book).

Striking Quality: The degree of sharpness evident on a coin will affect its value. Thus, an early coin with all details sharply struck, including the hair strands on Miss Liberty's head, the points of the stars, the feathers on the eagle, and the veins in the leaves, will sell for much more than one with flatly struck features. It is always the case that a sharply struck coin is more valuable than a weakly defined one. However, for certain early coins, sharply struck examples do not exist, so one cannot make this an absolute requirement in the search to complete a collection.

Centering: A well-centered coin is preferable to one struck slightly off center. Twentieth-century coins are usually well centered as a matter of course, but 18th and early 19th-century issues are apt to be poorly centered.

Planchet Quality: The presence of mint-caused adjustment marks, lamination areas, or other planchet defects will reduce a coin's value and, if strong or sharply defined, should be mentioned as part of a coin's description. Refer to our Dictionary of Numismatic Terms and our chapter on minting procedures for other information.

Aesthetic Appeal: Beauty is in the eye of the beholder, and what is a "beautiful" coin to one person may not be to another. Some collectors prefer attractive iridescent toning, while others prefer pieces to be brilliant or bright. Among collectors of copper coins, some prefer coins with an evenly toned brown surface, while others prefer a mixture of brown with original mint red. In general, a coin with excellent aesthetic quality is one which has a pleasing appearance, is free from marks or problems, and which for its grade is an exceptional or outstanding example.

Split Grades

Split grades are often used to more accurately describe a coin. It may be the case that the obverse of a coin is in a different grade than the reverse. As illogical as this may seem, in practice it does happen. For example, among Morgan dollars, the design of the obverse is such that the cheek of Miss Liberty is in high relief and is susceptible to scratches, scuffs, and marking when a coin comes into contact with others. By contrast the reverse is in shallow relief and is more protected by the rim, so that the same amount of mingling with other coins produces fewer marks on the reverse, and the marks on the reverse that do occur are often hidden in the complicated feather design of the eagle. A Morgan dollar (or other coin) which has an MS-63 obverse and MS-65 reverse can be described as MS-63/65. This is more accurate and conveys a better description of the coin than stating that the coin is MS-63, which isn't doing justice to the reverse, or incorrectly stating that the coin is MS-65, for this results in overgrading the obverse. In general, but not always, split grades are relatively close together. It would not be logical, for example, for a coin to have a Very Fine-30 obverse and an MS-63 reverse, for these grades are widely separated.

It is a matter of debate whether a coin can be About Uncirculated on one side and Uncirculated on the other. As no one knows the life experience of a coin, or whether a coin actually went into circulation, or whether what is perceived as rubbing or scuffing on a high surface was due to coin-to-coin contact in a bag, or was obtained in the channels of commerce, this argument will never be resolved. In general, if one side of a coin is graded, for example, as AU-58 because it shows very slight rubbing, and the other side shows no rubbing at all, it is permissible to grade the coin as AU-58/MS-60, meaning in this instance that the obverse is AU-58 and the reverse grades MS-60.

Among Proof coins, split grades are also seen on occasion. Years ago, coins were kept face-up in cabinets, so that the obverse of a coin sometimes acquired nicks, marks, or other hairlines, while the reverse remained relatively unimpaired. Thus, a coin can be described as being Proof-63/65, meaning the obverse is Proof-63 and the reverse is Proof-65.

The value of a split grade coin is closer to the lower grade than to the higher. Thus, if a coin has a market value of $100 in MS-63 grade and $200 in MS-65 grade, a coin with a split grade of MS-63/65 might be worth, say, $125, or closer to $100 than to $200. There are no rules in this regard, and each situation is different.

Sharpness and Grade

The quality of striking of a coin—whether a piece is sharply defined, weakly defined, or somewhere between—does not affect the grade, although it can affect the value. Indeed, there are numerous coins in American numismatics which are only known with shallow striking or definition. For example, there is probably no such thing as a sharply struck, well-defined half cent of the year 1797. And yet, if at the moment of striking, a piece had been removed from the dies by a gloved hand, and kept in perfect condition, with full mint color, ever since that time, it would be proper to designate it as MS-70. Dr. Sheldon noted concerning early copper cents: "A number of the early varieties are always found with certain portions of the coin weak—a result of injured or bent dies. Such coins, even when in Mint State, will lack some of their detail."

Returning to the example of the 1797 MS-70 half cent, a proper catalogue description, abbreviated for purposes of illustration, might be: "1797 half cent. MS-70, with characteristic light striking, and poor detail on the higher parts."

Although light striking is the rule among many early issues, among coins from the mid 19th century onward, sharply struck coins exist for most varieties, although in some instances sharply struck pieces are rare. Take for example the 1926-D Buffalo nickel. At the Denver Mint that year, the dies were spaced fairly wide apart, to prevent rapid die wear, so that the resultant coins are very flat appearing, with very little detail at the center of the obverse and reverse. A 1926-D Buffalo nickel with just a few scattered marks might be properly described as MS-65, but another piece, also technically MS-65, but described as "MS-65, sharply struck," might be worth many multiples of the former.

The mixing of striking characteristics with grade in order to create a grade which does not have to be further described is practiced by some. In other words, it is a practice of some to take an MS-65 coin which is weakly struck, and downgrade it to MS-63 or even MS-60, and say no more about it. However, this is unfair to the buyer, for the buyer would not know anything about the definition of design detail under such a method.

Various "bid" and "ask" prices are often linked to a combination of grade and value. For example, *The Coin Dealer Newsletter* specifically notes that certain prices given for MS-65 silver dollars, for example, are coins which not only are MS-65 but, in addition, are sharply struck. This additional requirement is often overlooked by collectors who assume that a published price is for *any* coin in a given grade, regardless of striking problems or defects.

Chapter 5

Grades and Prices

by Q. David Bowers

Grade vs. Price

Of the various considerations which help to determine the value of a coin, the grade of the piece is one of the most important factors. For many buyers in the coin field—particularly investors and buyers without knowledge or collecting interest—the grade of a given piece is often the only factor in their making a decision.

Bid prices from a copy of the *Coin Dealer Newsletter* show the vast differences in price a coin can have depending upon its grade (information used by permission):

1896-O Morgan Silver Dollar: VG-8 $7.50, F-12 $8, VF-20 $9, EF-40 $12, AU-50 $45, MS-60 $220, MS-63 $1,660, MS-64 $5,300, and MS-65 $30,000.

Using these prices it can be seen that in well-worn VG-8 grade an 1896-O dollar is worth $7.50, but in MS-65 preservation the value multiplies to $30,000. Along the way it is evident that a small difference in grade can make a big difference in price. For example, the difference in price from MS-64 at $5,300 and MS-65 at $30,000 is almost 6 to 1. In other words an MS-65 coin is worth about six times the price of an MS-64 coin.

It is obvious that great caution must be taken when buying coins at this level. If a coin is graded MS-65 but barely, and someone may later regrade it at MS-64, you can see there is a great potential for loss. Similarly, if you buy a very nice specimen of an MS-64 piece, one which challenges the MS-65 grade, it may be a true bargain at the MS-64 level—and may be a candidate for being graded even higher.

In addition, there is the consideration as to the *value received for the price paid*. If I were forming a collection I might well be satisfied with an MS-64 coin, assuming I could afford it, rather than paying a great deal more for a coin in just slightly better MS-65 preservation.

1923-S Monroe Doctrine Centennial Commemorative Half Dollar: EF-45 $26, MS-60 $33, MS-63 $95, MS-64 $280, MS-65 $2,025.

The 1923-S Monroe half dollar, the price structure of which is given above, is somewhat similar although at lower dollar levels. An MS-64 coin at $280 may well be a better buy than an MS-65 at $2,025, the latter being about eight times more expensive. Put another way, seven or eight MS-64 coins can be bought for the price of a single MS-65. If it were my money I would look seriously at a quality MS-64.

On the other hand there are coins for which a small difference in grade does not necessarily mean a large difference in price. An example provided by the 1936 Norfolk, Virginia, Bicentennial half dollar. Listings are as follows:

1936 Norfolk Half Dollar: EF-45 $300, MS-60 $325, MS-63 $340, MS-64 $360, MS-65 $375. It seems to go almost without saying that most serious numismatists would rather have an MS-65 coin at $375 than a worn EF-45 piece for $300. The explanation for this price structure is that this particular half dollar was primarily sold to collectors who saved them at the time of issue, and most have been carefully preserved since that time. None were put into circulation. Thus, most specimens that exist are in Mint State ranges. An EF-45 piece would be a *great rarity* because of this (although it would not have higher value as people desire better graded coins).

In recent years, particularly since about 1990, a number of the grading services have certified numerous pieces in grades above MS-65 such as MS-66, MS-67, MS-68, and MS-69. The guidelines the certification services use have never been defined in print, and it is my personal observation that quality can vary widely — what one person calls MS-68 another might call MS-66, and so on. As these words are being written, the market for higher graded (above MS-65) coins seems to lie primarily with investors, not with collectors. Almost any Proof set or commemorative coin issued in the past twenty or thirty years, if kept in its original Mint holder, is virtually in perfect condition today and is a candidate for some of these high grades. Confusion lies with interpretation and understanding of the market. Sometimes investors are mislead into paying high prices for modern coins certified as MS-68 or MS-69 because they do not know that most of them actually are in these grades. They have heard stories about how an early large cent from the 19th century, or a silver dollar from the 1860s, or some other *early* coin brought an astronomical price in a high grade, and they wrongly feel that the same philosophy translates to modern pieces.

The "investigate before you invest" philosophy will quickly shortcut any problems you may have in this regard. If you are not familiar with coins, by all means withhold purchasing them until you gain an understanding of market value, availability, and grading. In particular be aware of coins that are sold as potential investments by firms that have few if any serious numismatic credentials. A lot of telemarketing firms have latched upon coins as something to sell, and often price their pieces at *multiples* of what they are truly worth.

On the other hand, with a clear understanding of grading and current values, and with purchases made from recognized numismatic firms, you will be in a position to make intelligent purchases of quality coins, and in the process you will build a beautiful collection. Whether the collection will increase in value over the years depends on a number of factors including the national and world economy, cycles within the coin market, and popularity trends, but at least you will know that the coins you have are choice for the grade ranges involved.

When I wrote the introduction to the book, *Official ANA Grading Standards for U.S. Coins,* I inserted this paragraph:

> "A note concerning market values: it is important to know that grade *is only a part of* market valuation. Two silver dollars can each be in MS-65 grade but can differ widely in value. The average specimen of a certain date might be worth, for example, $800, while a weakly struck piece with an unappealing surface, but still MS-65, might be worth $400, and a sharply struck coin with beautiful toning might worth $1,000 or more. It is important not to rely on grading alone to determine the value of a coin, for the stated grade of a coin— even if determined by experienced professionals or by grading services—is only part of the story."

My advice about high-grade Mint State and Proof examples of coins which are not rarities: Let investors pay today's high prices for common coins, especially in grades over MS-65 and Proof-65. As noted in my earlier examples of the 1886-O Morgan silver dollar and 1923-S Monroe commemorative half dollar, often a coin in a slightly lower grade such as MS-64 can be a better value for the money than an MS-65 costing much more.

Sources of Pricing Information

Today's coin buyer has more pricing information available than anyone has ever had before. Indeed, there is so much information at hand that sometimes it is difficult to understand and digest it all. There is no single source that infallibly points the way to what price to pay. In all instances it is to be remembered that coins of hand-selected quality often sell for more than the prices listed. For some pricing sources, the values listed are for the *worst* examples of the grades indicated, meaning that coins are worth at least those values, and often even more.

The Direct Sales Department of Bowers and Merena Galleries uses the following sources, among others, but these are the primary ones (listed in alphabetical order):

Electronic Exchanges: We monitor certain of the computer networks linking dealers. These often have bid and ask prices for various coins. Prices are often erratic, and a coin with a bid price sight-unseen (which means the buyer guarantees to buy the coin no matter what its appearance may be) may be vastly lower than a quality piece in the same grade for which the buyer can make a before-purchase inspection. However, these exchanges do have some value, especially for more common coins traded in quantity or bulk groups of silver dollars, modern commemoratives, and the like. *The Certified Coin Dealer Newsletter* lists summaries of certain exchange transactions.

Auction Prices Realized: Results of actual sales at recent auctions are particularly useful in determining the value of scarce and rare coins of selected quality (assuming that the auction catalogues in question describe the surfaces, etc. of the pieces). Krause Publications issues a yearly study of coin auction prices, which is valuable not only for price levels but for the frequency of appearance of certain coins. In order to study auction prices effectively you must maintain a file of catalogues issued by various dealers and also gain knowledge of which firms have a practice of buying a significant percentage of the items listed.

Coin Dealer Newsletter: This weekly newsletter, first published in 1963, gives market levels for non-slabbed (raw) coins in many different series, and in grades from Good to MS-65 or Proof-65 (but not all grade ranges for all series). Listed each week are popularly traded series such as commemoratives and silver dollars.

Specialized series dating back to the late 19th century are detailed in the *Monthly Summary*, issued each month. The

Monthly Summary contains many superb in-depth articles about the rare coin market, collector and investor psychology, etc. Nickname: *Greysheet*.

Coin World: The "Trends" section is carefully researched and contains valuable pricing information on all series from 1793 to date.

Keith Zaner, editor of the "Trends" section of *Coin World*, posed these questions: 1. Just what do the values listed each week in "Trends" mean? 2. What do they indicate? His answers: "For better understanding, it may be easier to state what the Trends' section is not. Trends' values are not bid or ask prices. They are not the final price or one which is inflexible. Trends' values do represent 'ballpark' estimates or ranges of current retail values for rare coins. A single Trends' value is an established point from which a dealer, collector or investor can, if he chooses, deviate from to arrive at a market transaction price.

"For example, if a Trends' value of $5,000 is listed for a particular coin, it is reasonable to assume that a seller (dealer, investor or collector) may request a price above, at, or below that dollar amount. The same holds true for the buyer. Price is contingent upon many variables which interact with one another. The weighted variables are pertinent to determining price.

"If the seller wants $5,500, then that is well within the ballpark. Even at $6,000, availability and demand may dictate this greater increase.

"Trends' values are all listed at the lowest grade level within each grading category, with the exception of the Mint State and Proof listings. When the Very Fine-20 values are listed, the Trends' value is for a VF-20 coin. Coins which grade VF-25, VF-30, and VF-35 are worth more than the VF-20, but less than an Extremely Fine-40 coin. A VF-30 coin may or may not be worth a value which is the midpoint of EF-40 and VF-20. This is because of the many variables which affect and are integral in establishing the price of a rare coin. Perhaps most important, the market establishes Trends' values, not the Trends' editor.

"Trends' values are listed for coins which totally and by strict market standards meet the requirements at each grade level. Coins which are so-called borderline usually are and fall back to the next lowest grade level. The coin values in Trends' are for coins which do not exhibit any one of the many problems which may be a part of the coin's history. Problems such as harsh cleaning, heavy scratches, whizzing, rim or other surface damage can lower substantially the value of a coin, even though technically it is in a grade which may carry a much higher value.

"Color and eye appeal are important. If a coin has attractive color or better than average eye appeal, then it is reasonable to assume its market value may be greater than the Trends' value listed in that grade. Demand for top quality coins is increasing today. If the coin is dull for the grade, then the value will probably be less and so will the demand."

Dealers' Fixed Prices: Catalogues and advertisements of dealers provide a guide to what certain coins can actually be bought for in the marketplace. Of course, some prices may be unrealistically high, and listed prices which seem to be too low may be for undesirable coins, but by and large a great deal of information is available from these listings.

Experience: This may be the single most important factor used here at Bowers and Merena Galleries. Experience covers a wide variety of factors, including knowledge of market demand, the availability of other items of comparable quality (not only grade, but overall quality), etc. Experience is what makes a professional numismatist valuable to his clients.

Guide Book: A Guide Book of U.S. Coins, published annually, is a very valuable source of information concerning mintage figures, which varieties exist for which series, historical information, etc. Pricing data is very valuable for all except the most actively traded series. The book is prepared a year in advance, and the 1995-dated edition was released in July 1994. *The Guide Book* reports prices, it does not create them, so it can lag behind the market. Nickname: *Red Book.*

Numismatic News: The weekly "Coin Market" feature, edited by Bob Wilhite, is a valuable source of information, much like the

Coin World "Trends." For many series, "Coin Market" lists three prices, explained as follows:

Buy: What dealers pay to purchase coins for inventory or to wholesale to other dealers.

Bid: What dealers pay for coins, generally through other dealers on Teletype, which will sell immediately.

Sell: Average price realized for a coin sold at retail.

A recent listing contained the following spreads, as examples:

1893 Columbian 50c, MS-63: *Buy* $63, *Bid* $70, *Sell* $85.

1923-S Monroe 50c, MS-64: *Buy* $250, *Bid* $280, *Sell* $340.

1881-CC $1, MS-65: *Buy* $270, *Bid* $300, *Sell* $400.

1895-S $1, MS-60: *Buy* $835, *Bid* $925, *Sell* $1,150.

1922-S $1, MS-64: *Buy* $195, *Bid* $215, *Sell* $275.

Liberty Head type 5c, MS-63: *Buy* $65, *Bid* $70, *Sell* $90.

Barber type 25c, Proof-65: *Buy* $1,305, *Bid* $1,450, *Sell* $1,850.

Indian type $10, MS-63: *Buy* $880, *Bid* $980, *Sell* $1,100.

These are guidelines, and actual transactions may vary. For example, if I had a ready sale for a Proof Barber 25c at $1,850, and someone offered me one for $1,750, I wouldn't turn it down, to wait for the chance, which might never come, to obtain one for the listed "buy" price of $1,305 or the "bid" price of $1,450. On the other hand, if I had several dozen such coins in stock and envisioned no ready sale for them, I might not want to pay the "bid" price of $1,450, but would be a buyer only at some lower level. Further, if a coin was not aesthetically pleasing to me, I might not want it at any price.

The "Coin Market" feature offers excellent guidelines, and anyone wanting to know what an average Proof-65 Barber quarter is worth can certainly gain some ideas from the preceding spread.

Population Reports: Issued at regular intervals by PCGS and NGC, these reports show how many coins have been certified in various grades. They are not at all representative of the total population in existence of a certain issue, for few coins below MS-60 are submitted for common varieties, as it costs $20 to $25 or so to have a coin certified. As more and more coins are certified in the future, the populations will increase.

The popular practice of resubmitting coins has these two effects:

1. The same coin can appear twice (or more) and give the impression that a variety is more common than it actually is (one dealer I know submitted an MCMVII High Relief $20 four times before he was able to get the grade he wanted; this coin appears in the population report as four different listings, whereas in reality only one specimen is represented). In another instance a 1916-D dime (a valuable rarity) was resubmitted nearly two dozen times.

2. Proportionally, there are more higher-graded slabbed coins in existence than the data show, for many lower-grade listings which swell the report numbers do not exist, as they have been reslabbed at higher levels.

Population reports are quite valuable in determining the *relative rarity* of certain coins in higher grade levels. For example, if in a hypothetical situation the PCGS report lists 77 MS-65 examples, 17 MS-66 pieces, and 8 MS-67 specimens of a particular variety, if you own an MS-66 or MS-67 example, you have an item which will sell for a sharp premium above the MS-65 level.

Surface Characteristics

When I wrote the introduction to the *Official ANA Grading Standards for United States Coins* book, I stated that there are specific factors which establish the characteristics of a coin's surface. These can affect a coin's value, sometimes significantly. What appear as imperfections or marks on a coin can occur because of the following:

Characteristics of the Die Used to Strike the Coin: Before 1836, most dies were prepared by hand. The engraver, using a matrix or hub, punched in the portrait of Miss Liberty, the wreath or other device, and individual letters and numerals. Sometimes a tool would slip or an accident would occur, and unintended marks would appear on the die and be transferred to all coins struck from that die. A variety of 1795 silver dollar has a prominent "bar" behind the head, the result of an accident to the die. The die for a certain variety of 1804 half cent was apparently injured when a bolt from the coining press became loose, fell upon the lower die on the press, and was then forced against the bottom die when the top die came down. Many other examples can be given.

Clash marks are seen on many varieties of early coins and were caused by two dies coming together without an intervening planchet. An impression of the obverse die was made upon the reverse, and vice versa, so that any coin struck later from this die pair showed evidence of this accident. Clashed dies seem to be particularly common in the silver three-cent piece series, perhaps because the tiny planchets often slipped and were not easy to handle, but other series display them as well. A correspondent sent me a fine photograph of a modern Kennedy half dollar with prominent clash marks on the obverse, showing traces of the heraldic eagle design transferred from the reverse.

After a die was used for a period of time it was apt to become worn or to develop cracks. Such cracks were filled with metal from the planchets when coins were struck, causing raised ridges or irregular lines known as die breaks. These are typically irregular in outline and extend inward from the border, although particularly severe cracks can extend all the way across a coin from rim to rim. Breaks caused by metal chipping away from the edge of the die produced blobs of metal at the rim and are sometimes called "cud" breaks. Most die breaks do not affect the value of a coin either positively or negatively, although among certain early issues in which breaks are severe and an entire section of the die shows injury, resultant coins display partial or missing inscriptions and are often worth less than fully struck examples.

1937-D "3-Legged" Variety

As dies became worn, sometimes they were resurfaced by grinding, thus removing certain details. The 1937-D Buffalo nickel with three legs is believed to have been the result of one leg being partially rubbed away in the die by the use of a file or, as some texts say, an emery board. Liberty Seated half dollars such as 1845-0, 1846-0, and 1877-S are often seen with prooflike surfaces and with part of the drapery absent from Miss Liberty's elbow. When these dies were resurfaced, the drapery, being one of the lower relief features, was ground away. The grinding and resurfacing marks were covered up by polishing the dies, giving the coins prooflike surfaces.

Restrike of 1804 Cent

Sometimes dies were stored in damp circumstances, with the result that coins struck from them show evidence of rust pits on the die. Certain 1833 quarters, 1876-CC dimes, and other issues were struck from heavily rusted or even corroded dies. The so-called "restrike" 1804 large cent was struck from dies which had been left to the ravages of the elements for many years.

In general, die characteristics such as rust spots, breaks, accidental marks in the die, etc., are not specifically mentioned in coin descriptions, unless they are felt to affect the value. Certain varieties are especially popular due to their having been struck from problem dies. Among these are the 1795 half cent without pole to cap (the pole to the liberty cap on the obverse was ground away during die resurfacing, thus creating this distinctive variety), the 1801 AMERICA! silver dollar (a die mark, possibly a break, exists after the last letter in AMERICA and has the fanciful appearance of an "I"), and the 1796 LIKERTY half dime (a rather silly variety, for the "K" is simply a defective B). Often a die defect of years ago can translate into a highly prized collectors' item today!

No Pole to Cap Half Cent

Characteristics of the Planchet. Marks seen on the surface of a coin can be due to the quality of the original planchet used to produce the piece. During the process of preparing planchets, metal is rolled into long strips. Sometimes bubbles, laminations, and streaks occur which can be transferred to coins. It is not uncommon among early silver coins to see black or gray streaks, the result of carbon and other imperfections in the metal, such imperfections having been distended into streaks by the rolling process. Particularly notable laminations and streaks should be mentioned when a coin is described.

Adjustment marks are common on silver and gold coins of the late 17th and early 18th centuries and are a result of the legal requirement that such pieces be of a precise weight and value. It was not possible to consistently produce planchets of precisely the authorized weight, for such technology was not in place. It was realized that if the pieces were made too light, metal could not effectively be added, and such planchets would have to be remelted. The course pursued was to make the planchets slightly heavier than intended. Once this was done, the pieces were sent to ladies who worked at the Mint adjusting each piece. Each planchet was put on a scale, weighed, and then a file was drawn across the surface to remove any excess amount of metal. If the first filing did not suffice, then another pass with a file was used, perhaps in a different direction. The resultant planchet had parallel file grooves, ranging from light to heavy, on the surface. After this planchet was used for coinage, sometimes the file marks would not be obliterated, particularly toward the edge of the coin or on the higher parts of the coin's surface. Some adjustment marks are par for the course among silver and gold issues, particularly gold issues, of the 1790s and early 1800s, and are not usually mentioned in connection with the grade, although particularly extensive adjustment marks should be noted.

The metal from which planchets were made often had different characteristics. Collectors of early large cents know that issues of 1799, for example, almost always come with very dark brown or black coloration, due to the metal used, which came from various commercial sources. Cents of 1814 are often black, while cents dated 1836 are usually a pleasing chocolate brown color. Early Mint records indicate that freshly minted copper cents and half cents in some instances were dark, not brilliant, as they left the press. Among later coins, bronze Indian cents and Lincoln cents made at the San Francisco Mint in 1909 were struck on planchets made from an alloy giving the pieces a light yellow or straw color, rather than the normal red or orange surface, after striking.

During the preparation process, blank planchets are subjected to all kinds of rough treatment, and in this way acquire numerous abrasions, tiny nicks, etc. When the planchet is used to make a coin, if certain areas of the planchet are not fully impressed into the deepest recesses of the die so as to make the planchet metal flow against the die surfaces, it is the case the original marks on the planchet can still be seen on the coin.

This is a fine point of distinction, and most collectors and dealers are not aware of it. For this reason a softly struck Liberty Walking half dollar, for example, can have virtually flawless, frosty, lustrous fields but on the higher parts of the coin show nicks and marks from the original planchet.

Marks Acquired After a Coin is Struck

I have just described how marks, die breaks, evidence of die clashes, laminations, adjustment marks, and other attributes of dies and planchets can affect the appearance of a coin and are characteristic of a piece at the moment of striking. Now I address the grade or condition of a coin, which is determined by marks, abrasions, friction, and other evidences of contact which occur after a coin is struck. An explanation of the striking process is in order.

The typical minting procedure for a coin produced for circulation, known as a *business strike*, is as follows:

After the planchets are prepared they are put into a bin or hopper, from which they are jostled or, in early times, hand placed into a feeding tube on the coin press, which positions each planchet between the dies (certain types of modern coining presses have multiple dies and use more than one planchet at a time). The coin is struck when the top die, being movable, is forced down on to the planchet, which is resting on the bottom die. The metal is squeezed upward and downward into the recesses of the obverse and reverse dies and outward into a restraining device, called a collar (which imparts to the coin the characteristics of the collar, typically plain or reeded in modern times). No care is taken to strike coins with needle-sharp detail, as the object is to produce coins as rapidly as possible. As a result, some coins are carelessly or weakly struck (more about this later).

After a typical coin is struck it is mechanically ejected from the dies, and slides down a chute or tube into a metal box, where other coins are heaped on top of it. By this time the coin, if viewed under magnification, is apt to have a number of nicks and abrasions.

From this point the coin is dumped from the metal box into a large storage bin, during which process the piece comes into contact with numerous other coins. As each bin becomes full it is taken to another area of the mint where it is unloaded, and the pieces are fed into a mechanical counting machine, which jostles the coins even more and imparts additional abrasions. The coins are then run at high speed through a mechanical counter, after which they go through a chute and are dumped into cloth bags and stored. The cloth bags are not handled with care and are piled upon each other. The bags are put into a safe storage place, until they are called for to be shipped to Federal Reserve banks or other locations, to which places they are typically shipped by motor freight.

Coin Storage and Distribution. The Federal Reserve system distributes bags of coins to member banks, which often place them into circulation either as loose change or by running them through mechanical devices which count and wrap them (creating bank-wrapped rolls).

To this point the typical coin has not been in circulation, nor has it been touched by human hands. However, it may have acquired enough nicks, scratches, and abrasions that it would barely make the grade MS-60! I remember seeing a bank-wrapped roll of 1958 Philadelphia Mint Jefferson nickels in which there wasn't a single coin I would grade better than AU-58, and yet the coins had never been in circulation! Perhaps from a technical viewpoint they were indeed Uncirculated, but no knowing buyer would have bought them as such.

The larger and heavier a coin is, the more susceptible it is to receiving abrasions and other handling marks. When in the 1970s the General Services Administration distributed Treasury-stored Morgan dollars, which had been kept by the government since the 1870s and 1880s in many instances, purchasers often found that the coins were heavily nicked, scratched, and abraded, although the pieces had never been out of government hands and had not circulated. Such issues as 1893-CC and 1895-S in particular are usually seen with extensive contact marks.

In general, a Morgan silver dollar, a Saint-Gaudens double eagle, a Liberty Seated half dollar, or some other large and relatively heavy coin will have more bagmarks and abrasions than a small, light coin such as a silver three-cent piece, half dime, dime, or gold dollar.

Sharpness or Weakness of Strike

The sharpness or lightness of strike can affect a coin's value and, in recent times (for views have changed on this), a coin's grade. Consider as an example the 1941-S Liberty Walking half dollar. Nearly all known specimens, probably 95% or more, have the details on the skirt of Miss Liberty and on the central part of her figure weakly defined. Had you or I been present at the San Francisco Mint in 1941, and at the moment of striking had we taken with a gloved hand a typical 1941-S half dollar from the dies, it would have exhibited a flatness not unlike that observed on a coin which had spent several years in circulation. And yet the coin would have received no nicks, scratches, abrasions, or handling marks, for the newly minted specimen had yet to come into contact with anything else except a gloved hand. From a technical viewpoint, I suggest that a proper numismatic description of this coin, if offered in an auction catalogue, should be something like this:

"1941-S Liberty Walking half dollar. MS-70 from the standpoint of handling and contact marks; there is absolutely no evidence of such. However, in keeping with nearly all other known specimens of the variety, the details of Miss Liberty are lightly defined on the higher areas, giving the coin a flat appearance at the center. This coin is worth an MS-63 price."

However, this view would not be in step with prevailing numismatic philosophy. Instead, the piece would be downgraded to, say, MS-63 to reflect its market level, with nothing said about the weakness of strike.

Let me describe another specimen of an 1941-S half dollar. This second coin is one that is among the very few examples that were sharply struck at the time of issue. This particular coin was produced at the San Francisco Mint in 1941, was ejected from the dies, slid down a chute into a box, was dumped in a hopper, bagged, run through a counting machine, passed through the Federal Reserve system, sent to a bank, put in a paper-wrapped roll, and, finally, was acquired by a collector. The piece never circulated, but yet there were sufficient nicks, abrasions, and other evidences of handling to merit the piece being called MS-

63 by today's grading standards. Thus we have a second MS-63 half dollar, this one sharply struck. From my viewpoint, the ideal description for the second piece would be as follows:

"1941-S Liberty Walking half dollar. MS-63. Sharply struck, and one of relatively few known specimens to exhibit needle-sharp details on the higher areas."

If you were a bidder in one of my firm's auction sales, and these two 1941-S half dollars were listed, even though both might be worth MS-63 money, in your mind's eye you would be able to differentiate the two coins and determine which one you wanted. For the price of an MS-63 coin, would you prefer an MS-70 coin with virtually perfect surfaces, but which is flatly struck, or would you prefer a sharply struck piece with abrasions? This is up to you. However, you would have the opportunity to make an informed choice.

Today, in the world of certified coins, both pieces would simply be slabbed as MS-63, with no further distinction made. So few people seem to care about such distinctions as sharpness of strike that it may be a waste of print to give the elaborate descriptions of 1941-S half dollars just cited.

Interestingly, when a coin is weakly defined on the higher parts, such as the 1941-S half dollar, or numerous Buffalo nickels struck at branch mints during the 1920s, or Standing Liberty quarters of the 1920s, 1921 Peace silver dollars, or other issues which are often seen flatly struck, this had nothing to do with the wear of the dies. Uninformed cataloguers have often said that such pieces have been struck from "worn dies," but this is not the case. When dies wear, they do so in areas which are subjected to the greatest amount of lateral metal flow on the planchet—areas such as the fields and near the rims. The deepest recesses of the dies receive the least amount of wear.

The weakness just described in the 1941-S half dollar was due to inadequate die spacing. During the production process, technicians at the Mint endeavored to space the dies closely enough together that the coins would strike up properly, but wide enough apart that excessive die wear and breakage would not occur. If the dies were spaced too closely together, after the metal filled the deepest recesses in the dies and filled the reeding or other areas of the collar, it had to have some place to go, and would either create a wire rim around the coin (a knifelike edge caused by metal extruding between the die and collar) or would cause die breakage. The simple solution was (and still is at the various mints) to space the dies slightly further apart than the optimum. In that way if a planchet was slightly overweight it would not cause breakage, nor would a wire rim be created.

Technicians were more careless than usual at the San Francisco Mint in 1941, and the half dollar dies were spaced too far apart. Another outstanding case is the 1926-D Buffalo nickel. Probably 99 out of 100 known specimens are flatly struck. Except for their lustrous surfaces, such coins give every indication that they have been in circulation for years! Similarly, nearly all known 1926-D Standing Liberty quarters have Miss Liberty's head weakly struck.

Apropos of grading in recent times, I have heard it said that unless a coin is sharply struck, it cannot be graded any higher than MS-65. This rule seems to be in general use now. Thus, an 1892-O silver dollar, to mention an issue which is often lightly struck, cannot be graded higher than MS-65 even if it has virtually perfect fields. An extremely sharply struck 1892-O is a candidate for any and all higher grades, depending on the amount of nicks and abrasions it has received.

In other instances of weak striking, dies were created with the designs in low relief. Certain 1793 half cents have the words HALF CENT lightly impressed on the reverse, for these words were shallowly impressed into the dies. Sesquicentennial commemorative half dollars dated 1926 are often indistinct, simply because the design was executed in shallow relief without bold features. In other instances, particularly among issues of the 1790s, improperly hardened dies tended to sink in certain areas, resulting in evident weakness on coins struck from these dies.

In still other instances, the obverse and reverse dies were not completely parallel to each other, with the result that the coins of a particular variety can be weak on one side and sharp on the other. The 1794 large cent known as the "Shielded Hair" variety is very deeply impressed on the left side of the obverse and lightly impressed on the right side. United States silver dollars of the same year, 1794, are typically seen lightly impressed at the lower left of the obverse (and corresponding part of the reverse) and sharp at the opposite area of the coin, at the upper right.

"Market Grade"

For purposes of evaluating a coin—once you are relatively familiar with numerical grades—the "market grade" concept may be useful. Indeed, this sometimes appears in print. As an example, certain members of the Early American Coppers Club assign what are called net grades to early large cents. Often a large cent (minted 1793-1857) may have a certain technical or numerical grade such as EF-45, but may show oxidization or light corrosion. Looking at such a coin, an observer might make a value judgment that it is worth the market price of an F-15 piece. Accordingly, such a piece would be listed in an expanded description as: Sharpness of EF-45, but with lightly oxidized surface. Market value net F-15." This concept is a bit esoteric and involves a combination of market knowledge, experience with the series at hand, and grading principles, and is primarily in the purview of advanced collectors and dealers. However, it is worth mentioning as you may come across it.

Increasingly there has been a tendency to assign just a single number to describe a coin's grade, and to use no additional adjectives at all. Bumps, scratches, hairlines, etc. are factored into the grade, and, as noted, an EF-40 coin with problems can be slabbed simply as a VF-20, or a Proof-65 coin with lint marks can be encapsulated as a Proof-63 or some lesser grade. Do you remember my theoretical MS-70 1941-S half dollar, weakly struck, being called MS-63? Unquestionably, using just a single number simplifies things, as it makes prices easier to compute.

Under this philosophy, a coin is assigned a single grade number which reflects its market price, not necessarily its technical grade. This is a departure from the grading systems outlined in the 1970s and 1980s in *Photograde* and the *Official ANA Grading Standards for United States Coins* books.

To expand on the subject, I give three illustrations:

1895-S Silver Dollar: Obverse heavily bagmarked, numerical grade for the obverse alone: MS-60. Reverse lightly bagmarked (fewer bagmarks than on the obverse, due to the protective nature of the letters and eagle design), numerical grade for the reverse alone: MS-63.

> *Old Grading System*: 1895-S $1. MS-60/63. Obverse heavily bagmarked (information a collector might want to know).

> *New Grading System*: 1895-S $1. MS-60.

In both instances the coins have the same market value. Only the descriptions are different.

1872 Proof Liberty Seated Half Dollar: Cleaned long ago, and now with a few light hairlines in the fields. Deep gray, almost black, toning in blotches (information a collector might want to know). Numerical grade: Proof-64.

> *Old Grading System*: 1872 Liberty Seated half dollar. Proof-64. Deep gray, almost black, toning in blotches.

> *New Grading System*: 1872 50c. Proof-63. (Some would still call it Proof-64 and not mention the blotches, etc.; a low-end 64.)

In both instances the coins have the same market value. Only the descriptions are different.

1926-D Buffalo Nickel: MS-65 from the standpoint of wear, but very weakly struck, as usual for this variety.

> *Old Grading System*: 1926-D 5c. MS-65, weakly struck, as usual for this variety.

> *New Grading System*: 1926-D 5c. MS-63.

In both instances the coins have the same market value. Only the descriptions are different.

In today's market coin buyers are often confronted with just numbers, with little in the way of adjectival descriptions to indicate what a coin looks like. I suggest that you, as an astute buyer, determine in advance what any coins you want to purchase do indeed look like, for once you own them, you may have to look at them for many years! If, as extensively mentioned by the *Certified Coin Dealer Newsletter*, alert *dealers* pay higher prices for coins they can see before making a commitment, perhaps you should also!

Chapter 6

United States Coin Grades
The Photograde System

How to Use Photograde

Every major type of United States coin from the first year of regular federal issues, 1793, through the 1950s is represented in this book. Different condition ranges are pictured and described. It is easy to check any coin with the uniform arrangement of pictures and descriptions. Simply follow the pictures with your coin until you come to the closest match. Then check the description beside that picture. Do the same for both the obverse and reverse. The terminology used to describe each condition is in the most basic, most concise form for quick reference.

1793 Half Cent

About Good (AG-3)

Obverse: Head and wreath will be distinct; a partial date must show. "LIBERTY" may not be distinct.

Reverse: The wreath will be almost complete but only a few letters of the legend will be readable.

Good (G-4)

Obverse: Most of the lettering and design will be readable. The outline of the head will stand out boldly.

Reverse: The wreath will be complete. Half of the legend will be readable.

Very Good (VG-8)

Obverse: Some hair detail will be visible. Date will be bold.

Reverse: The legend will be complete but some letters will be weak.

Note: The words "HALF CENT" were weakly struck on certain varieties and should not be used to determine condition.

Fine (F-12)

Obverse: About one-third of the hair detail will show. All the lettering will be clear.

Reverse: The leaves and berries in the wreath, although complete, will be quite flat.

1793 Half Cent

Very Fine (VF-20)

Obverse: At least half of the hair detail will be sharp. The hair ribbon will be distinct.

Reverse: The leaves in the wreath will be stronger but will not show leaf detail.

Extremely Fine (EF-40)

Obverse: All major hair detail will show but will be worn on the high spots at the shoulder and to the right of the ear.

Reverse: the leaves in the wreath will show some detail and appear more rounded.

About Uncirculated (AU-50)

Obverse: Only a trace of wear will show on Liberty's cheek and to the right of her ear.

Reverse: Most leaves will show full detail although some may not be fully struck up.

Liberty Cap Half Cents
1794-1797

About Good (AG-3)

Obverse: The head will be outlined but worn smooth. Lettering will be worn; date will partially show.

Reverse: A partial wreath and legend will show but will be very weak.

Good (G-4)

Obverse: Most of "LIBERTY" will show. The date will be readable but may be quite weak.

Reverse: The wreath will be quite weak. At least half of the legend will be readable.

Note: The words "HALF CENT" were weakly struck on certain varieties and should not be used to determine condition.

Very Good (VG-8)

Obverse: Some hair detail will show by the shoulder. "LIBERTY" will be strong but the date still may be weak (depending on the variety).

Reverse: The wreath will be complete. The legend will be complete (except on certain die varieties which were always weakly struck).

Fine (F-12)

Obverse: About one-third of Liberty's hair will show plainly. The date will be clearly defined.

Reverse: The wreath will be bold but worn flat. There will not be any leaf detail.

Liberty Cap Half Cents
1794-1797

Very Fine (VF-20)

Obverse: At least half of Liberty's hair will be distinct.

Reverse: About half of the leaves will be individually separated but still show no detail.

Note: Weakness on only one area of a coin is probably due to the design or striking of that particular variety. This should be disregarded when determining condition. (This is applicable to any early United States coin.)

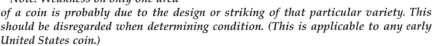

Extremely Fine (EF-40)

Obverse: Almost full hair detail on Liberty's head, but definite wear will show around the ear and neck.

Reverse: All of the leaves will be separated from each other. There will be some leaf detail on the bottom leaves.

About Uncirculated (AU-50)

Obverse: Wear will show only on the highest waves of hair around the ear and neck.

Reverse: Most of the leaves will show full detail and will be worn on the highest points only.

- 63 -

Draped Bust Half Cents
1800-1808

About Good (AG-3)

Obverse: An outline of the head and a partial date will show.

Reverse: A partial wreath and legend will show.

Good (G-4)

Obverse: The head will be sharply outlined. All lettering will be readable although weak.

Reverse: The wreath will be complete. There may be wear on the tops of some of the letters of the legend.

Very Good (VG-8)

Obverse: Hair detail will begin to show at the shoulder. "LIBERTY" will be strong.

Reverse: The lettering will be complete. The wreath will be bold but worn flat.

Fine (F-12)

Obverse: Drapery on the bust will show but be worn at the top. About half of the hair detail will be visible.

Note: The bridge over the letters "RTY" is caused by a die break. Die breaks do not alter the condition of a coin.

Reverse: A few leaves will be separated and show some detail.

Draped Bust Half Cents
1800-1808

Very Fine (VF-20)

Obverse: About two-thirds of the hair detail will be visible. The top line of the drapery will be complete to the hair.

Reverse: Almost all the leaves will be separated. The bottom leaves will show some detail.

Extremely Fine (EF-40)

Obverse: All hair detail will show but will be weak above the forehead and ear. The drapery will be well defined.

Reverse: Most of the leaves will show detail.

About Uncirculated (AU-50)

Obverse: There will be slight wear on the hair above the forehead and to the left of the ear.

Reverse: There will only be a trace of wear on the highest points of the leaves.

Turban Head Half Cents
1809-1836

About Good (AG- 3)

Obverse: The rim will be worn down to the stars and date. Some "LIBERTY" letters may show.

Reverse: Only a partial legend will show. "HALF CENT" will be readable.

Good (G-4)

Obverse: The head will be well outlined and may show a full "LIBERTY." Date will be bold.

Reverse: The rim will be worn down to the tops of the letters but all lettering will be readable.

Very Good (VG-8)

Obverse: Hair detail and the ear will begin to show. There must be a full "LIBERTY."

Reverse: All letters will be complete. The wreath will be bold but worn almost flat.

Fine (F-12)

Obverse: Two-thirds of the hair detail will show. Hair curl on the neck will show clearly although the hair above the forehead will be worn. "LIBERTY" will be strong.

Reverse: Most of the leaves will be separated; a few will show detail.

Turban Head Half Cents
1809-1836

Very Fine (VF-20)

Obverse: All hair will show but will be weak around Liberty's face and below the ear.

Reverse: About half of the leaves will show detail and all will be separated.

Extremely Fine (EF-40)

Obverse: Full hair will show but there will be wear on the higher points.

Reverse: All the leaves will show some detail.

About Uncirculated (AU-50)

Obverse: The hair detail will be very sharp with only a trace of wear on the higher points.

Reverse: Slight wear will show on only the highest points of the top leaves.

Half Cent Token
1837

Fine (F-12)

Obverse: There will be a trace of detail on the eagle's wings.

Reverse: The leaves in the wreath will be separated and a few will show detail.

Note: *This token is rarely found in conditions below Fine.*

Very Fine (VF-20)

Obverse: About two-thirds of the eagle's wings will show feathers.

Reverse: About half of the leaves will show detail.

Extremely Fine (EF-40)

Obverse: All the eagle's feathers will show but will be worn on the high points.

Reverse: More detail will show on the leaves.

About Uncirculated (AU-50)

Obverse: There will be a trace of wear only on the highest points of the feathers. The top of the eagle's right wing may be flatly struck.

Reverse: Slight wear will be visible on only the highest points of the leaves.

Braided Hair Half Cents
1840-1857

Very Good (VG-8)

Obverse: Full "LIBERTY" but "L" will be weak. About half of the hair detail will be visible but not sharp.

Reverse: The wreath will be outlined with the leaves worn flat.

Fine (F-12)

Obverse: Hair cord will be sharp. Hair around the face will be outlined but worn.

Reverse: Most leaves will be separated and begin to show some detail.

Very Fine (VF-20)

Obverse: All hair detail will show but will be weak about the ear and by the neck.

Reverse: About half of the leaves will show detail.

Extremely Fine (EF-40)

Obverse: All hair detail will be well outlined with wear only on the higher points.

Reverse: All the leaves will be detailed but will show definite wear.

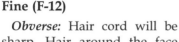  

About Uncirculated (AU-50)

Obverse: Only the slightest trace of wear will show on Liberty's hair above her ear.

Reverse: Slight wear will be visible on only the highest points of the leaves.

Chain Large Cent
1793

Fair (Fair-2)

Obverse: Identifiable as to type by the distinct head type. No date will show.

Reverse: The chain must show.

About Good (AG-3)

Obverse: The head will be well worn. A partial date must show.

Reverse: The chain will be well defined. Some of the legend will be readable.

Good (G-4)

Obverse: The head will be outlined although worn flat. The date will show but may be worn at the bottom or weakly struck.

Reverse: Most of the legend will be readable, including the denomination "ONE CENT."

Very Good (VG-8)

Obverse: The date will be full. Head will be well outlined.

Reverse: All the lettering will be readable although some letters will be weak.

Chain Large Cent
1793

Fine (F-12)

Obverse: The tips of Liberty's hair will be well outlined but the other two-thirds of her hair will be worn smooth.

Note: The head almost always comes weakly struck. This must be considered when grading Chain cents.

Reverse: The chain and center lettering will be bold. All other lettering will be distinct.

Very Fine (VF-20)

Obverse: About half of Liberty's hair will show detail. Her ear may not show on the average weakly struck piece.

Reverse: The chain and center lettering will be very bold.

Extremely Fine (EF-40)

Obverse: Hair below Liberty's ear and above her head will show definite wear.

Reverse: The links of the chain will be well rounded with wear showing only on the high points.

About Uncirculated (AU-50)

Obverse: Wear will be visible only on the highest points of hair around Liberty's face.

Reverse: Only a trace of wear will be visible on the highest points of the chain.

Wreath Large Cent
1793

About Good (AG-3)

Obverse: A partial date must show.

Reverse: Most of the wreath will be clear with only a few letters visible.

Good (G-4)

Obverse: Head will be worn completely flat. Date and "LIBERTY" will show but may be weak.

Reverse: The rim may be worn down into some of the letters.

Very Good (VG-8)

Obverse: All letters and date will show clearly. One-third of the hair detail will be distinct.

Reverse: All the lettering will be clear (but some may be weak due to striking).

Fine (F-12)

Obverse: All lettering and date will be sharp. About half of the hair detail will be visible.

Reverse: The wreath will be well outlined but flat. Lettering will be sharp.

Wreath Large Cent
1793

Very Fine (VF-20)

Obverse: About two-thirds of the hair detail will show.

Reverse: The beaded border will be sharp. Leaves will be separated but worn flat.

Extremely Fine (EF-40)

Obverse: There will be wear on the highest points of hair from the forehead to the shoulder.

Reverse: There will be a slight roundness to the leaves.

About Uncirculated (AU-50)

Obverse: The hair detail will be complete but worn on the highest points to the left of the ear and neck.

Reverse: The leaves will be well rounded with wear only on the highest points.

Liberty Cap Large Cents
1793-1796

About Good (AG-3)

Obverse: The head and some lettering will be visible. Date will be readable although weak.

Reverse: Most of the wreath will be clear with only a few letters visible.

Good (G-4)

Obverse: The head will be well defined. Most of the lettering and date will be clearly readable.

Reverse: The rim may be worn down into some of the letters (which will be visible but weak).

Note: The words "ONE CENT" were weakly struck on certain varieties and should not be used to determine condition.

Very Good (VG-8)

Obverse: Some hair detail will show. All lettering will be distinct.

Note: There may be weakness in spots due to the methods of striking these early coins.

Reverse: All the lettering will be clear.

Fine (F-12)

Obverse: About half of Liberty's hair will show clearly.

Reverse: The wreath will be well outlined but flat.

Liberty Cap Large Cents
1793-1796

Very Fine (VF-20)

Obverse: The hair behind Liberty's ear and above her forehead will be worn but the rest of the hair will be detailed.

Reverse: The leaves will be separated but show very little detail.

Extremely Fine (EF-40)

Obverse: All major hair detail will be visible with wear only on the high spots.

Reverse: The leaves will be well defined with some leaves showing detail.

About Uncirculated (AU-50)

Obverse: All the hair detail will be strong but will show a trace of wear on the higher points.

Reverse: Leaf detail will be quite distinct with only slight wear visible.

Draped Bust Large Cents
1796-1807

About Good (AG-3)

Obverse: The head will be outlined and the date will be readable but weak.

Reverse: Half of the lettering will be visible.

Good (G-4)

Obverse: The head will be distinctly outlined.

Reverse: All the letters will be readable although the rim may be worn down into some of them because of uneven striking.

Very Good (VG-8)

Obverse: About one-third of the hair detail will show. The date will be bold.

Reverse: All letters will show. The wreath will be outlined but show no detail.

Fine (F-12)

Obverse: About two-thirds of the hair detail will show. The hair will be smooth above Liberty's forehead, the top of her head, and to the left of her neck.

Reverse: Some of the leaves will show individual separation.

Draped Bust Large Cents
1796-1807

Very Fine (VF-20)

Obverse: Almost all the hair will be visible but will be worn flat on the higher points.

Note: Coins made over 150 years ago were often unevenly struck or have imperfections that cannot be standardized in any grading book.

Reverse: Each individual leaf will be well defined with little detail showing.

Extremely Fine (EF-40)

Obverse: Full hair will show but have wear on the tips of the curls and to the right of Liberty's forehead.

Reverse: Most of the leaves will show detail but will be worn on all the high spots.

About Uncirculated (AU-50)

Obverse: All hair detail will be sharp. There will only be a trace of wear on the highest points of hair.

Reverse: All the leaves will show detail or be well rounded. Wear will show only on the very highest points.

Turban Head Large Cents
1808-1814

About Good (AG-3)

Obverse: The rim will be worn down into the stars. Date will be readable but weak.

Reverse: Half of the lettering will be visible.

Good (G-4)

Obverse: The date and stars will be clear. The head will be distinctly outlined. A partial "LIBERTY" may show.

Reverse: All the letters will be readable although the rims may be worn down into some of them because of uneven striking.

Very Good (VG-8)

Obverse: About one-third of the hair detail will show, and the ear will be visible. A full "LIBERTY" will show.

Reverse: All the letters will show although some may be weakly struck. The wreath will be flat but well defined.

Fine (F-12)

Obverse: About two-thirds of the hair will show, but weakly. Hair around the face will be worn almost smooth. The ear will be sharp.

Reverse: The top leaves of the wreath will be worn flat.

Turban Head Large Cents
1808-1814

Very Fine (VF-20)

Obverse: All the hair will show but be quite weak in detail.

Reverse: The top leaves and bow will show some detail.

Extremely Fine (EF-40)

Obverse: Full hair will show but will be worn above the eye, above "LIBERTY," and on the tips of the curls.

Reverse: The high points of the leaves will show wear.

About Uncirculated (AU-50)

Obverse: The hair will be quite sharp with only a trace of wear on the higher points.

Note: The hair above "LIBERTY" was usually weakly struck.

Reverse: There will be only a trace of wear on the highest points of the leaves and wreath bow.

Coronet Type Large Cents
1816-1839

About Good (AG-3)

Obverse: The rim will be worn down into the stars. The date will be readable but weak.

Reverse: Half of the lettering will be visible.

Good (G-4)

Obverse: The date and the stars will be clear. The head will be distinctly outlined. A partial "LIBERTY" may show.

Reverse: All the letters will be readable although the rim may be worn down into some of them because of uneven striking.

Very Good (VG-8)

Obverse: About one-third of the hair detail will be visible. The hair cords will begin to show. "LIBERTY" will be full.

Reverse: All the letters will show strongly. The wreath will be flat but well defined.

Fine (F-12)

Obverse: Most of the major hair detail will be visible. The hair cords will show weakly.

Reverse: The top leaves and the wreath bow will be worn flat.

Coronet Type Large Cents
1816-1839

Very Fine (VF-20)

Obverse: The hair will be worn flat on the higher points. Both hair cords will show plainly.

Reverse: The top leaves and bow will show some detail.

Extremely Fine (EF-40)

Obverse: The hair will be sharp with weakness showing only above the forehead and at the highest point on top of the head. Hair cords will stand out sharply.

Reverse: The highest points of the leaves will show wear.

About Uncirculated (AU-50)

Obverse: Only a trace of wear will be visible on the higher points of the hair.

Reverse: There will be a trace of wear only on the highest points of the leaves and wreath bow.

Braided Hair Large Cents
1839-1857

About Good (AG-3)

Obverse: The date and stars will be weak but visible.

Reverse: Half of the lettering will be visible.

Good (G-4)

Obverse: The date and stars will be clear. The head will be distinctly outlined. A partial "LIBERTY" may show.

Reverse: All the lettering will be readable although the rim may be worn down to the tops of some of the letters.

Very Good (VG-8)

Obverse: "LIBERTY" will be readable but "L" and "I" will be weak. About one-third of the hair detail will be clear.

Reverse: All the lettering will show strongly. The wreath will be flat but well defined.

Fine (F-12)

Obverse: About two-thirds of the hair detail will show. Hair above the eye will show but be worn. Beaded hair cords will be sharp.

Reverse: The top leaves will be worn flat.

Braided Hair Large Cents
1839-1857

Very Fine (VF-20)

Obverse: All hairlines will be complete but some will be weak, especially on top of the head. Hair above the eye and the beaded hair cords will be well defined.

Reverse: The top leaves will show some detail.

Extremely Fine (EF-40)

Obverse: The hair above the ear will be slightly worn.

Reverse: The highest points of the leaves will show wear.

About Uncirculated (AU-50)

Obverse: Only a trace of wear will show on the highest points of the hair above the ear and eye.

Reverse: There will be a trace of wear only on the highest points of the leaves and wreath bow.

Flying Eagle Cents
1856-1858

About Good (AG-3)

Obverse: The date will be weak but readable.

Reverse: The rim will be worn down into the wreath.

Good (G-4)

Obverse: The lettering and the date will be readable although the rim may be worn down to the tops of the letters.

Reverse: The wreath will be completely outlined but worn flat.

Very Good (VG-8)

Obverse: About one-third of the feathers on the eagle will show but will be weak.

Reverse: The wreath will show some detail but be worn smooth on top.

Fine (F-12)

Obverse: About half of the feathers on the eagle will show. The detail of the eagle's head will be very clear.

Reverse: More detail will appear on the wreath.

Flying Eagle Cents
1856-1858

Very Fine (VF-20)

Obverse: About three-quarters of the feathers will show sharply. The eagle's tail feathers will be complete. There will be considerable flatness on the eagle's breast.

Reverse: The ends of the leaves will be worn smooth.

Note: The words "ONE CENT" are sometimes weak due to striking.

Extremely Fine (EF-40)

Obverse: There will be wear on the eagle's breast and left wing tip. All other details will be sharp.

Reverse: There will be wear on the high points of the leaves and ribbon bow.

About Uncirculated (AU-50)

Obverse: There will be only a trace of wear on the eagle's breast and left wing tip.

Note: Weakness of lettering and date may appear on some 1857 cents due to striking.

Reverse: Only a trace of wear will show on the highest points of the leaves and bow.

Indian Head Cents
1859-1909

About Good (AG-3)

Obverse: The rim will be worn down well into the letters. The date will be weak but readable.

Reverse: The rim will be worn down into the wreath.

Good (G-4)

Obverse: The outline of the Indian will be distinct. "LIBERTY" will not show on the headband. The rim may be worn down to the tops of the letters.

Reverse: The wreath will be completely outlined but worn flat.

Very Good (VG-8)

Obverse: A total of any three letters of "LIBERTY" will show. This can be a combination of two full letters plus two half letters as not all dates of Indian cents wore uniformly.

Reverse: The wreath will begin to show some detail.

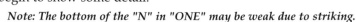

Note: The bottom of the "N" in "ONE" may be weak due to striking.

Fine (F-12)

Obverse: A full "LIBERTY" will be visible but it will not be sharp.

Reverse: The top part of the leaves will be worn smooth. The ribbon bow will show considerable wear.

Indian Head Cents
1859-1909

Very Fine (VF-20)

Obverse: A full sharp "LIBERTY" will be visible even though there is some wear. The feathers will be worn on the tips.

Note: Indian cents cannot be graded by the diamond designs on the ribbon as this feature was not always sharply struck.

Reverse: There will be more detail in the leaves and ribbon bow.

Extremely Fine (EF-40)

Obverse: There must be a full sharp "LIBERTY." The ends of the feathers (except on certain weakly struck issues, such as 1859-1864 copper-nickel pieces) will be sharply detailed.

Reverse: There will be wear on the high points of the leaves and ribbon bow.

About Uncirculated (AU-50)

Obverse: Only a trace of wear will show on the highest points such as above the ear and the lowest curl of hair.

Reverse: Only a trace of wear will show on the highest points of the leaves and ribbon bow.

Lincoln Head Cents
1909 to Date

About Good (AG-3)

Obverse: The rim will be worn down into the letters. Date and mintmark will be weak but readable.

Reverse (1909-1958): The rim will be worn down into the letters and the wheat stalks.

Good (G-4)

Obverse: Letters in the legend may be touching the rim. The date will be full.

Reverse (1909-1958): The wheat stalks will be worn smooth but distinctly outlined.

Very Good (VG-8)

Obverse: All letters in the legend will be sharp and clear. A few hair details will begin to show.

Reverse (1909-1958): About half of the lines in the upper wheat stalks will show.

Fine (F-12)

Obverse: Lincoln's ear and bow tie will be clearly visible.

Reverse (1909-1958): The parallel lines in the upper wheat stalks will show plainly and be separated even though worn. One side or the other may show a weak area at the top of the stalk.

Lincoln Head Cents
1909 to Date

Very Fine (VF-20)

Obverse: The ear and bow tie will be sharp. All of Lincoln's hair will be visible but worn. The cheek and jaw details on Lincoln's face will show clearly.

Reverse (1909-1958): The lines in the wheat stalks will be full and will show no weak spots.

Extremely Fine (EF-40)

Obverse: There will be wear only on the high points of Lincoln's head and face.

Reverse (1909-1958): The lines in the wheat stalks will be very bold and clearly defined.

Note: Many "D" and "S" coins of the 1920s are weakly struck, and should be graded by the best side. 1922 "Plain" is very weakly struck and lacks sharp detail, even in the higher grades.

About Uncirculated (AU-50)

Obverse: Only the slightest trace of wear will show on the high points of Lincoln's cheek and jaw.

Reverse (1909-1958): Only a trace of wear will show on the wheat stalks.

Two-Cent Pieces
1864-1873

About Good (AG-3)

Obverse: The rim will be worn down into the date and wreath.

Reverse: Half of the lettering will be visible.

Good (G-4)

Obverse: The date will be clear. A partial "IN GOD WE TRUST" must show.

Reverse: All the lettering will be visible although a few letters may be weak.

Very Good (VG-8)

Obverse: The motto words "IN GOD" and "TRUST" will show clearly. There will be a slight trace of the word "WE."

Reverse: All the lettering will be bold. Half of the wheat grains will show.

Fine (F-12)

Obverse: The motto "IN GOD WE TRUST" will show completely, but "WE" will be quite weak.

Reverse: Almost all the wheat grains will show.

Two-Cent Pieces
1864-1873

Very Fine (VF-20)

Obverse: The entire motto, including "WE," will be easily readable.

Note: The horizontal lines in the shield may not be complete even on higher grades due to striking.

Reverse: All the wheat grains will show plainly.

Extremely Fine (EF-40)

Obverse: The full motto will be boldly readable. The leaves will show considerable detail especially at the bottom.

Reverse: The high points of the wreath and ribbon will show wear.

About Uncirculated (AU-50)

Obverse: There will be only a trace of wear on the high points of the design, such as the tips of the leaves, the arrow points, and the word "WE."

Reverse: There will be a trace of wear only on the highest points of the wreath and ribbon.

Nickel Three-Cent Pieces
1865-1889

About Good (AG-3)

Obverse: The rim will be worn down into some of the letters.

Reverse: The rim will be worn down into the wreath.

Good (G-4)

Obverse: The rim will be worn down to the tops of the letters.

Reverse: The leaves in the wreath will be flat and only a few will be separated.

Very Good (VG-8)

Obverse: There will be a full rim. Very little hair detail will show.

Reverse: There will be a full rim. About half of the leaves will be separated from each other.

Fine (F-12)

Obverse: About one-third of the hair detail will show.

Note: This coin usually comes with weak hair detail over the ear even on higher-grade coins.

Reverse: All the leaves will be separated. Some of the lines will show weakly in the Roman numeral III.

Nickel Three-Cent Pieces
1865-1889

Very Fine (VF-20)

Obverse: Two-thirds of the hair detail will show plainly.

Reverse: The lines will be sharper.

Note: This coin often comes with weakly struck lines even on higher-grade pieces.

Extremely Fine (EF-40)

Obverse: The upper hair and lower curls should be very sharp.

Reverse: All the lines will be boldly visible in at least one figure of the Roman numeral III. There will be wear only on the tips of the leaves.

About Uncirculated (AD-50)

Obverse: Only the slightest trace of wear will show on the hair curls and the hair above the forehead.

Reverse: Only a trace of wear will show on the wreath and Roman numeral III.

Shield Nickels
1866-1883

About Good (AG- 3)

Obverse: The rim will be worn down into the letters and wreath.

Reverse: The rim will be worn down into the letters.

Good (G-4)

Obverse: The date and all letters should be clear although the rim may be worn down to the tops of the letters. Leaves will be flat.

Reverse: The rim will be worn down to the tops of the letters.

Very Good (VG-8)

Obverse: The leaves will show slight detail. Some of the horizontal lines in the shield will show.

Reverse: There will be a full rim.

Note: The numeral "5" may be weak in spots due to striking. This should not affect the grade.

Fine (F-12)

Obverse: Individual leaves will be separated but worn smooth halfway from the tips to the center of the leaves.

Reverse: The stars, with a few lines showing, will be very bold.

Shield Nickels
1866-1883

Very Fine (VF-20)

Obverse: The leaves will be more defined and clearly separated.

Reverse: Most of the lines in the stars will be complete.

Note: If some stars are strong and some weak, determine grade by the strong ones. (Certain issues have all stars weakly struck, in which case determine grade by the obverse only.)

Extremely Fine (EF-40)

Obverse: The leaves will stand out in bold relief with most of the center lines showing clearly.

Note: The horizontal lines in the shield may be incomplete because of striking even on higher grades and should not affect the grading.

Reverse: The strongest stars will show full sharp lines.

About Uncirculated (AU-50)

Obverse: Only a trace of wear will show on the tips of the leaves and on the highest points of the shield.

Reverse: The stars will show only a trace of wear (but may be weak, as noted, due to striking).

Liberty Head Nickels
1883-1913

About Good (AG-3)

Obverse: The rim will be worn down into the stars and/or the date.

Reverse: The figure "V" and the wreath will be visible.

Good (G-4)

Obverse: Liberty will be outlined but the legend "LIBERTY" will not show on her headband.

Reverse: The rim may be worn down to the tops of the letters. "E PLURIBUS UNUM" will be barely visible.

Very Good (VG-8)

Obverse: A total of any three letters of "LIBERTY" must show. This could be a combination of two full letters plus two half letters as not all dates of Liberty nickels wore uniformly.

Reverse: The wreath will be sharply outlined. "E PLURIBUS UNUM" will show weakly.

Fine (F-12)

Obverse: A full "LIBERTY" must be readable, including the letter "I." About half of the hair detail will be visible.

Reverse: Detail will begin to appear in the wreath. "E PLURIBUS UNUM" will be strong.

Liberty Head Nickels
1883-1913

Very Fine (VF-20)

Obverse: "LIBERTY" will be complete and bold. The hair will show about 75% detail.

Reverse: Partial detail will show on the leaves of the wreath and the ear of corn.

Extremely Fine (EF-40)

Obverse: "LIBERTY" will be very bold. All the details will be visible but may be weak on the high points above the ear and forehead.

Reverse: There will be wear on the high points of the wreath and ear of corn.

About Uncirculated (AU-50)

Obverse: There will be only the slightest trace of wear on the highest portion of the hair above the ear and forehead.

Reverse: There will be only a trace of wear on the highest portions of the wreath.

Buffalo Nickels
1913-1938

About Good (AG-3)

Obverse: The rim will be worn down well into the letters. Only a partial date will show, but date must be recognizable.

Reverse: The rim will be worn down into the letters.

Good (G-4)

Obverse: The rim will be worn down into the tops of the letters of "LIBERTY." The date will be readable but some of the numbers will be well worn.

Reverse: The rim may be worn down into the tops of the letters. The horn need not show.

Very Good (VG-8)

Obverse: The rim may touch the tops of the letters of "LIBERTY". The date will be distinct.

Reverse: There will be a full rim. Half of the horn will show. The bison's back will be almost smooth.

Fine (F-12)

Obverse: "LIBERTY" will be separated from the rim. The date will be very bold.

Reverse: Two-thirds of the horn will show. The major detail on the bison's back will show.

Buffalo Nickels
1913-1938

Very Fine (VF-20)

Obverse: The hair braid and cheek will show some detail but be flat on the high spots.

Reverse: There will be a full horn but the top may not be well outlined. The hair on the bison's head will be well worn.

Extremely Fine (EF-40)

Obverse: The hair braid and face details on the Indian are now very bold with only slight wear on the high points.

Reverse: A full sharp horn will show. The tail will show on the hip. Flat spots of wear will show on the head, upper front leg, and on the hip.

About Uncirculated (AU-50)

Obverse: There is only the slightest trace of wear on the highest point of the cheek.

Reverse: There will be only a trace of wear on the highest points of the upper front leg and hip. The tail will be sharp.

Note: Certain issues, particularly "D" and "S" mint issues of the 1920s, often come with weakly struck horn, tail, and "LIBERTY" even on Uncirculated specimens. 1926-D is particularly noted for such weaknesses.

Jefferson Nickels
1938 to Date

Good (G-4)

Obverse: The rim will be worn down to the tops of the letters. The head will be worn flat.

Reverse: Monticello will be worn smooth.

Very Good (VG-8)

Obverse: The rim will be worn down to the tops of the letters. Only the hair on the back of the head will show detail.

Reverse: The four main pillars of Monticello will show but be very weak.

Fine (F-12)

Obverse: About half of the major hair detail will show. The cheek will be worn flat.

Reverse: The two outer pillars will be well outlined. The two inner pillars will show but may not be complete from top to bottom.

Very Fine (VF-20)

Obverse: About three-quarters of the major hair detail will show.

Reverse: All four pillars will be well defined. The archway above the pillars will show major detail.

Jefferson Nickels
1938 to Date

Extremely Fine (EF-40)

Obverse: All the hair detail will show but will be worn on the high points. The cheekbone will be well rounded but show wear.

Reverse: All details on Monticello will show except the triangle in the arch above the pillars.

About Uncirculated (AU-50)

Obverse: There will be a trace of wear on the cheekbone and higher points of the hair.

Reverse: All details on Monticello will be sharp, including the triangle. There will be only a trace of wear on the highest points.

Note: The steps on Monticello will be full only on very well-struck pieces and should command a premium price.

Silver Three-Cent Pieces
1851-1873

About Good (AG-3)

Obverse: About half of the lettering will show.

Reverse: The rim will be worn down well into the stars.

Good (G-4)

Obverse: The rim may be worn down into a few letters and part of the date.

Reverse: The rim will be worn down to the tips of the stars.

Very Good (VG-8)

Obverse: The letters and date will be full. The shield in the center of the star may not be fully outlined.

Reverse: The stars will be well outlined and separated from the rim.

Fine (F-12)

Obverse: The shield will be complete.

Reverse: The design in the "C" will be more distinct.

Silver Three-Cent Pieces
1851-1873

Very Fine (VF-20)

Obverse: The star will be bold but show definite signs of wear on the high points and tips.

Reverse: The design in the "C" will be separated inside the circles.

Extremely Fine (EF-40)

Obverse: The star and shield will be very bold.

Reverse: The design in the "C" will now be well rounded.

About Uncirculated (AU-50)

Obverse: The star will show only a trace of wear on the top of each star point.

Note: The center of the shield may be weak due to striking on some pieces.

Reverse: Only a trace of wear

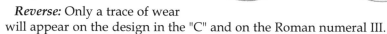

will appear on the design in the "C" and on the Roman numeral III.

Flowing Hair Half Dimes
1794-1795

About Good (AG-3)

Obverse: The rim will be worn down into the stars, legend, and/or date.

Reverse: The rim will be worn down well into the lettering and design.

Good (G-4)

Obverse: The bust will be outlined but will not show detail. The date, stars, and lettering will be readable.

Reverse: The rim will be worn into the tops of a few letters. The eagle will be outlined but show no detail.

Very Good (VG-8)

Obverse: Some detail will show on the ends of the hair. The major facial details will show.

Reverse: All the letters will be fully visible. The wings will show a few feather details.

Fine (F-12)

Obverse: About half of the major hair detail will show.

Reverse: A few more feathers will show in the wings. The leaves will be worn flat.

Flowing Hair Half Dimes
1794-1795

Very Fine (VF-20)

Obverse: The hair above Liberty's forehead will be outlined and will show major details.

Reverse: About half of the feathers will show. The leaves will be well rounded but show no detail.

Extremely Fine (EF-40)

Obverse: All the hair detail will show. There will be wear only on the high waves of hair.

Reverse: Most of the feathers will show in the wings.

Note: Because of striking, the breast rarely comes with full feather detail even on Uncirculated specimens. Some specimens have weakly struck wing feathers as well.

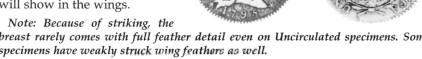

About Uncirculated (AU-50)

Obverse: Only a trace of wear will be visible on the high waves of hair around the face and ear.

Note: There may be weakness due to striking on the hair behind the ear.

Reverse: Only a trace of wear will appear on the head and top edges of the eagle's wings.

Draped Bust Half Dimes
1796-1805
(For 1800-1805 reverses see
Draped Bust Dimes 1796-1807)

About Good (AG-3)

Obverse: The rim will be worn down into the stars, "LIBERTY," and/or the date. The head will be worn flat.

Reverse: The rim will be worn down well into the letters and design.

Good (G-4)

Obverse: The rim will be worn down to the tops of the stars. A few letters of "LIBERTY" may be worn. Head will be well outlined.

Reverse: The rim will be worn down to the tops of some of the letters. The eagle will be outlined but show no detail.

Very Good (VG-8)

Obverse: About one-quarter of the hair detail will show, mostly in the lower curls. Some evidence of drapery lines will show.

Reverse: All the letters will be fully visible.

Fine (F-12)

Obverse: About half of the hair detail will show.

Reverse: Some feathers will show in the wings.

Draped Bust Half Dimes
1796-1805
*(For 1800-1805 reverses see
Draped Bust Dimes 1796-1807)*

Very Fine (VF-20)

Obverse: About three-quarters of the hair detail will show.

Note: Drapery lines across Liberty's bust cannot be used to determine grade as they vary greatly in sharpness from coin to coin because of striking.

Reverse: About half of the wing feathers will show.

Extremely Fine (EF-40)

Obverse: All the major detail of the hair will show. Wear will be visible to the left of the forehead.

Reverse: Most of the feathers will show in the wings.

Note: The breast feathers are rarely visible because of striking, even on high-grade specimens.

About Uncirculated (AU-50)

Obverse: Only a slight trace of wear will be visible on Liberty's bust, shoulder, and hair left of her forehead.

Note: Hair may be flat to the left of Liberty's neck due to striking.

Reverse: Only a trace of wear will appear on the head and top edges of the wings.

Capped Half Dimes
1829-1837

About Good (AG-3)

Obverse: The rim will be worn down into the stars and/or date. The head will be worn smooth.

Reverse: About half of the lettering will be visible.

Good (G-4)

Obverse: The head will be flat. At least half of "LIBERTY" will be readable.

Reverse: All the lettering will be complete. The eagle will be flat. There may not be a full "E PLURIBUS UNUM."

Very Good (VG-8)

Obverse: There will be a full "LIBERTY." About half of the hair detail will be visible.

Reverse: "E PLURIBUS UNUM" will be complete. There will be a few feathers showing in the eagle's left wing.

Fine (F-12)

Obverse: The lower drapery folds will be sharp. About three-quarters of the hair detail will show.

Reverse: About half of the feathers in the eagle's wings will show.

Capped Half Dimes
1829-1837

Very Fine (VF-20)

Obverse: All the major details of the hair will show, except the curl on the neck. The ear and drapery clasp will show clearly.

Reverse: Three-quarters of the feathers will show. The neck and right leg will show considerable wear.

Extremely Fine (EF-40)

Obverse: All the hair will be sharp with wear only on the highest curls. The curl on the neck will show.

Reverse: All the feathers will show but will be worn on the highest points. The edges of both wings will be worn.

About Uncirculated (AU-50)

Obverse: There will be only a trace of wear on the highest points of the hair above the forehead and ear.

Reverse: There will be only a trace of wear on the eagle's claws, neck, and along the edges of the wings.

Note: The right wing of the eagle and the center of "E PLURIBUS UNUM" may be flat due to striking.

Half Dimes (No Stars)
1837-1838

About Good (AG-3)

Obverse: The rim will be worn down into the field and may be worn into the date and/or head.

Reverse: About half of the lettering will be visible.

Good (G-4)

Obverse: There will be a full outline of Liberty. The shield will be worn smooth.

Reverse: The rim will be worn down to the tops of some of the letters.

Very Good (VG-8)

Obverse: A total of any three letters of "LIBERTY" will be visible on the shield.

Reverse: There will be a full rim. The leaves in the wreath will be outlined but not well defined.

Fine (F-12)

Obverse: There will be a full "LIBERTY" (including the letters "BE") on the shield, but it will not be sharp.

Reverse: The leaves will be separated but little detail will show.

Half Dimes (No Stars)
1837-1838

Very Fine (VF-20)

Obverse: "LIBERTY" will be sharp. Only the deepest folds of Liberty's gown will be visible.

Reverse: About half of the leaves will show detail.

Extremely Fine (EF-40)

Obverse: There will be wear on Liberty's breast and legs.

Reverse: All the leaves will show detail but will be worn on the ends.

About Uncirculated (AU-50)

Obverse: Only a trace of wear will appear on Liberty's breast and knees.

Note: The horizontal lines of the shield often come weak, even on higher grades.

Reverse: Only a trace of wear will be visible on the ribbon bow and the tips of the leaves.

Liberty Seated Half Dimes
1838-1859

About Good (AG-3)

Obverse: The rim will be worn down into the date and/or stars.

Reverse: About half of the lettering will be visible.

Good (G-4)

Obverse: There will be a full outline of Liberty. The shield will be worn smooth.

Reverse: The rim will be worn down to the tops of some of the letters.

Note: Half dimes of 1838-1859 are usually seen with the reverse weaker than the obverse by at least one grade. This is due to the shallower die relief of the reverse.

Very Good (VG-8)

Obverse: A total of any three letters (can be two full letters plus two half letters) of "LIBERTY" will be visible on the shield.

Reverse: There will be a full rim. The leaves in the wreath will be outlined but not well defined.

Fine (F-12)

Obverse: There will be a full "LIBERTY" on the shield, but it will not be sharp.

Reverse: The leaves will be separated but will have little detail.

Liberty Seated Half Dimes
1838-1859

Very Fine (VF-20)

Obverse: "LIBERTY" will be sharp. Only the deepest folds of Liberty's gown will be visible.

Reverse: About half of the leaves will show detail.

Extremely Fine (EF-40)

Obverse: There will be wear on Liberty's head, breast, and legs.

Reverse: All the leaves will show detail but be worn on the ends.

About Uncirculated (AU-50)

Obverse: Only a trace of wear will appear on Liberty's breast and knees.

Note: The clasp of Liberty's gown may be weak due to striking and therefore cannot be used to determine condition.

Reverse: Only a trace of wear will be visible on the ribbon bow and the tips of the leaves.

Liberty Seated Half Dimes
1860-1873

About Good (AG-3)

Obverse: The rim will be worn down into the letters and/or date.

Reverse: About half of the letters and/or design will be worn away.

Good (G-4)

Obverse: There will be a full rim. "LIBERTY" will not show.

Reverse: There will be a full rim. The wreath will be worn flat.

Very Good (VG-8)

Obverse: A total of any three letters (can be two full letters plus two half letters) of "LIBERTY" will be visible.

Reverse: Approximately half of the major detail will show in the wreath.

Fine (F-12)

Obverse: There will be a full "LIBERTY" but it will not be sharp. Only the deepest folds of Liberty's gown will be visible.

Reverse: All the major detail will be visible but will show definite wear.

Liberty Seated Half Dimes
1860-1873

Very Fine (VF-20)

Obverse: "LIBERTY" will be sharp. More detail will be visible on the upper folds of Liberty's gown.

Reverse: Wear will be apparent on the top half of the bottom leaves.

Extremely Fine (EF-40)

Obverse: There will be wear on Liberty's head, breast, and legs.

Reverse: There will be wear on the ends of the leaves and ribbon bow.

Note: There may be weakness due to striking at the top of the wreath. This weakness should not alter the grade of the coin.

About Uncirculated (AU-50)

Obverse: Only a trace of wear will appear on Liberty's breast and knees.

Reverse: Only a trace of wear will be visible on the ribbon bow and the tips of the leaves.

Draped Bust Dimes
1796-1807
(For 1796-1797 reverses see
Draped Bust Half Dimes 1796-1805)

About Good (AG-3)

Obverse: The rim will be worn down into the stars, date, and/or "LIBERTY."

Reverse: The rim will be worn down well into the legend and design.

Good (G-4)

Obverse: The rim may be worn down to the tops of the stars and legend. Head will be well outlined but worn flat.

Reverse: The rim will be worn down to the tops of some of the letters. The eagle will be clear but will show no detail.

Very Good (VG-8)

Obverse: About one-third of the hair detail will show. Some drapery lines will be visible.

Note: On these early dimes some areas may show more wear than others due to uneven striking. This should not alter the grade of the coin.

Reverse: A few feathers will show in the eagle's wings. A partial "E PLURIBUS UNUM" will show.

Fine (F-12)

Obverse: About half of the hair detail will show.

Reverse: About half of the features will show. "E PLURIBUS UNUM" may have a few weak letters.

Draped Bust Dimes
1796-1807
(For 1796-1797 reverses see
Draped Bust Half Dimes 1796-1805)

Very Fine (VF-20)

Obverse: About three-quarters of the hair detail will show.

Reverse: About three-quarters of the feathers will show and will be sharp.

Extremely Fine (EF-40)

Obverse: Almost all the hair detail will be visible, but portions may not be sharp due to striking.

Reverse: Wear will appear on the breast, tail, and at the ends of the wings.

About Uncirculated (AU-50)

Obverse: Only a trace of wear will be visible on Liberty's shoulder and the highest points of hair.

Reverse: Only a trace of wear will appear on the breast, tail, and at the tips of the wings.

Note: There may be weakness near the rims (especially on 1807 coins) due to striking. This should not affect the overall grade of the coin.

Capped Dimes
1809-1837

About Good (AG-3)

Obverse: The rim will be worn down well into the stars and/or date. The head will be worn smooth.

Reverse: The rim will be worn down well into the letters.

Good (G-4)

Obverse: The rim may be worn down to the tops of the stars (usually only on one side). The head will be well outlined.

Reverse: All the letters will be readable; a few of them may be weak.

Very Good (VG-8)

Obverse: A total of any three letters (can be two full letters plus two half letters) of "LIBERTY" will be visible. The rim will be full.

Reverse: All the letters will be sharp. A partial "E PLURIBUS UNUM" will show.

Fine (F-12)

Obverse: A full "LIBERTY" will show. The ear will be visible.

Reverse: There will be a full "E PLURIBUS UNUM." About half of the eagle's feathers will show.

Capped Dimes
1809-1837

Very Fine (VF-20)

Obverse: "LIBERTY" will be very sharp. About two-thirds of the hair will show.

Reverse: "E PLURIBUS UNUM" will be sharp. Almost all the feathers will show, but wear will be visible on the high points.

Extremely Fine (EF-40)

Obverse: All the hair will show but will be worn on the highest points of the curls and around the face.

Reverse: Wear will be visible on the highest points of the feathers, claws, and neck.

About Uncirculated (AU-50)

Obverse: Only a trace of wear will show on the shoulder and the hair above the ear and forehead.

Note: The clasp of Liberty's wrap may be weak due to striking and therefore can not be used to determine grade.

Reverse: Only a trace of wear will be visible on the eagle's neck, left claw, and the tips of the wings.

Dimes (No Stars)
1837-1838

About Good (AG-3)

Obverse: The rim will be worn down into the field and may be worn into the date and/or head.

Reverse: About half of the lettering will be visible.

Good (G-4)

Obverse: There will be a full outline of the Liberty seated figure. The shield will be worn smooth.

Reverse: The rim will be worn down to the tops of some of the letters.

Very Good (VG-8)

Obverse: A total of any three letters (can be two full letters plus two half letters) of "LIBERTY" will be visible on the shield.

Reverse: There will be a full rim. The leaves in the wreath will be outlined but not well defined.

Fine (F-12)

Obverse: There will be a full "LIBERTY" (including the letters "BE") on the shield, but it will not be sharp.

Reverse: The leaves will be separated but will show little detail.

Dimes (No Stars)
1837-1838

Very Fine (VF-20)

Obverse: "LIBERTY" will be sharp. Only the deepest folds of Liberty's gown will be visible.

Reverse: About half of the leaves will show detail.

Extremely Fine (EF-40)

Obverse: There will be wear on Liberty's breast and legs.

Reverse: All the leaves will show detail but will have wear on the ends.

About Uncirculated (AU-50)

Obverse: Only a trace of wear will appear on Liberty's breast and knees.

Note: The horizontal lines of the shield are often weak, even on higher grades, due to striking.

Reverse: Only a trace of wear will be visible on the ribbon bow and the tips of the leaves.

Liberty Seated Dimes
1838-1860

About Good (AG-3)

Obverse: The rim will be worn down into the date and/or stars.

Reverse: About half of the lettering will be visible.

Good (G-4)

Obverse: There will be a full outline of Liberty. The shield will be worn smooth.

Reverse: All the lettering will be full and sharp. The wreath will be worn flat.

Note: 1838-1860 Liberty Seated dimes are usually seen with the reverse weaker than the obverse by at least one grade. This is due to the shallower die relief of the reverse.

Very Good (VG-8)

Obverse: A total of any three letters (can be two full letters plus two half letters) of "LIBERTY" will be visible on the shield.

Reverse: The leaves in the wreath will be outlined but not well defined.

Fine (F-12)

Obverse: There will be a full "LIBERTY" on the shield, but it will not be sharp.

Reverse: The leaves will be separated but will not show much detail.

Liberty Seated Dimes
1838-1860

Very Fine (VF-20)

Obverse: The letters in the word "LIBERTY" will be sharp. Only the deepest folds of the Liberty seated figures gown will be visible.

Reverse: About half of the leaves will show detail.

Extremely Fine (EF-40)

Obverse: There will be wear on Liberty's head, breast, and legs.

Reverse: All the leaves will show detail but will have wear on the ends.

About Uncirculated (AU-50)

Obverse: Only a trace of wear will appear on Liberty's breast and knees.

Note: The clasp of Liberty's gown may be weak due to striking (rather than wear) and cannot be used to determine condition.

Reverse: Only a trace of wear will be visible on the ribbon bow and the tips of the leaves.

Liberty Seated Dimes
1860-1891

About Good (AG-3)

Obverse: The rim will be worn down into the letters and/or the date.

Reverse: The rim will be worn down into the wreath.

Good (G-4)

Obverse: There will be a full rim. "LIBERTY" will not show.

Reverse: The wreath will be well outlined but will be worn flat.

Very Good (VG-8)

Obverse: A total of any three letters (can be two full letters plus two half letters) of "LIBERTY" will be visible.

Reverse: Individual leaves will be outlined but show very little detail.

Fine (F-12)

Obverse: There will be a full "LIBERTY" but it will not be sharp. The deepest folds of Liberty's gown will be visible.

Reverse: All the major detail will be visible but will show definite wear.

Liberty Seated Dimes
1860-1891

Very Fine (VF-20)

Obverse: "LIBERTY" will be sharp. More detail will be visible on the upper folds of Liberty's gown.

Reverse: Sharper detail will appear on the leaves of the wreath.

Extremely Fine (EF-40)

Obverse: There will be wear on Liberty's head, breast, and legs.

Reverse: There will be wear only on the high points of the wreath.

About Uncirculated (AU-50)

Obverse: Only a trace of wear will appear on Liberty's breast and knees.

Reverse: Only a trace of wear will be visible on the tips of the leaves.

Note: There may be weakness at the top of the wreath due to striking. This weakness should not alter the condition of the coin.

Barber Dimes
1892-1916

About Good (AG-3)

Obverse: The rim will be worn down into the letters and/or date.

Reverse: The rim will be worn down into the wreath.

Good (G-4)

Obverse: The letters will be complete. The head will be well outlined but will be worn smooth.

Reverse: The wreath will be outlined but worn flat.

Very Good (VG-8)

Obverse: A total of any three letters (can be two full letters plus two half letters) of "LIBERTY" will show.

Reverse: Individual leaves will be outlined but will show very little detail.

Fine (F-12)

Obverse: There will be a full "LIBERTY" on the head but it will not be sharp. The top of the wreath will be well outlined but the bottom will be worn.

Reverse: All the major detail will be visible but will show major wear.

Barber Dimes
1892-1916

Very Fine (VF-20)

Obverse: "LIBERTY" will be sharp. The wreath will be well outlined at both top and bottom.

Reverse: Sharper detail will appear on the leaves of the wreath.

Extremely Fine (EF-40)

Obverse: The edges of the band on which the word "LIBERTY" appears will be distinct. The wreath will be bold. There will be wear above the forehead.

Reverse: There will be wear only on the high points of the wreath.

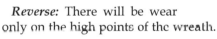

About Uncirculated (AU-50)

Obverse: Only a trace of wear will appear on the hair above the forehead, the tips of the leaves in the wreath, and the cheek bone.

Reverse: Only a trace of wear will be visible on the tips of the leaves.

Mercury Dimes
1916-1945

About Good (AG-3)

Obverse: The rim will be worn down halfway into the letters and date. Head will be worn smooth.

Reverse: The rim will be worn halfway into the letters and will touch the bottom of the mintmark (if any).

Good (G-4)

Obverse: The rim will touch the tops of the letters and the bottom of the last digit in the date. The wing will be flat.

Reverse: The rim will be worn down to the tops of the letters. The fasces will be worn smooth.

Very Good (VG-8)

Obverse: All the letters and the date will be clear of the rim. There will be a few feathers on the wing.

Reverse: The rim will be full. Half of the vertical lines in the fasces will show.

Fine (F-12)

Obverse: The rim will be sharp. About half of the feathers of the wing will be visible. Hair braid around the face will be worn smooth at the bottom.

Reverse: All the vertical lines will show but not sharply. The two diagonal bands will show across the fasces but will be worn smooth in the middle.

Mercury Dimes
1916-1945

Very Fine (VF-20)

Obverse: About three-quarters of the feathers will be visible. The hair braid will show more detail.

Reverse: All the vertical lines will be sharp. The two diagonal bands will be complete across the fasces.

Extremely Fine (EF-40)

Obverse: All the feathers will show but will be worn on the high points. Hair braid will be well detailed.

Reverse: The two diagonal bands will be raised across the fasces. The center horizontal bands will be sharp but not separated.

About Uncirculated (AU-50)

Obverse: Only a trace of wear will be visible on the hair braid and at the connection of the wing to the head.

Reverse: Only a trace of wear will appear in the center of the diagonal bands. The center horizontal bands will show only a trace of wear.

Roosevelt Dimes
1946 to Date

Good (G-4)

Obverse: There will be a full rim. Hair will be worn smooth. The ear will be worn flat.

Reverse: The rim will be worn down to the tops of the letters. The torch will be worn smooth.

Very Good (VG-8)

Obverse: About one-quarter of the hair will show.

Reverse: Only the lines at the side of the torch will show.

Fine (F-12)

Obverse: Half of the hair will show. The ear will be sharp.

Reverse: Half of the lines in the torch will show.

Very Fine (VF-20)

Obverse: Most of the major detail of the hair will be visible but worn on the high spots and around the face.

Reverse: Two-thirds of the lines in the torch will show.

Roosevelt Dimes
1946 to Date

Extremely Fine (EF-40)

Obverse: All the hair detail will show but will have slight wear to the right of the forehead and above the ear. The ear will show complete detail.

Reverse: All the lines in the torch will show. The flame will be well defined.

About Uncirculated (AU-50)

Obverse: Only a trace of wear will show on the cheekbone and on the hair above the ear.

Reverse: Only a trace of wear will show on the tops of the leaves and the high point of the flame.

Twenty-Cent Pieces
1875-1878

About Good (AG-3)

Obverse: The rim will be worn down into the stars.

Reverse: The rim will be worn well down into the letters.

Good (G-4)

Obverse: There will be a full rim. The shield will be worn smooth.

Reverse: There will be a full rim. The eagle will be worn almost smooth.

Very Good (VG-8)

Obverse: One or two letters of "LIBERTY" will show.

Note: "LIBERTY" is raised on the 20-cent piece instead of incused as on most other Liberty Seated coins. Therefore, different grading standards must be used for the 20-cent coin.

Reverse: About half of the feathers will show on the eagle. The center of the breast will be worn smooth.

Fine (F-12)

Obverse: Most of the word "LIBERTY" will show (with no more than 2 1/2 letters missing), but will be very weak in spots. The major details of Liberty's gown will show.

Reverse: Almost all the feathers will show. There will be a smooth spot in the center of the eagle's breast.

Twenty-Cent Pieces
1875-1878

Very Fine (VF-20)

Obverse: There will be a full "LIBERTY." Liberty's gown will show considerable detail.

Reverse: All the features will be visible but will show wear on the high spots.

Extremely Fine (EF-40)

Obverse: "LIBERTY" will be very sharp. There will be wear on the breast and legs.

Reverse: There will be wear on the eagle's breast, left leg, and tops of the wings.

About Uncirculated (AU-50)

Obverse: Only a trace of wear will appear on the head, breast, and knees.

Reverse: Only a trace of wear will appear on the eagle's breast and tops of the wings.

Note: The top of the eagle's right wing often (especially on 1875-55) appears flat, even on Uncirculated coins, due to striking.

Draped Bust Quarters
1796-1807
(For 1796 reverse see
Draped Bust Dollars 1795-1804)

About Good (AG-3)

Obverse: The rim will be worn down well into the stars and "LIBERTY."

Reverse: The rim will be worn down well into the lettering and design.

Good (G-4)

Obverse: The rim may be worn down to the tops of a few letters and/or stars. The head will be worn smooth.

Reverse: The rim will be worn down into the tops of some of the letters. The eagle's wings will be worn smooth.

Very Good (VG-8)

Obverse: The head will be well outlined with the top and bottom curls distinct. No hair detail will show around the face or neck.

Reverse: A few feathers will show in the wings. A partial "E PLURIBUS UNUM" will show.

Fine (F-12)

Obverse: About half of the major hair detail will show. There will be hair detail around the ear and to the left of the neck.

Reverse: About half of the

eagle's feathers will show. About half of "E PLURIBUS UNUM" will show.

Draped Bust Quarters
1796-1807
(For 1796 reverse see
Draped Bust Dollars 1795-1804)

Very Fine (VF-20)

Obverse: About two-thirds of the hair detail will show.

Reverse: Three-quarters of the eagle's feathers will be visible. "E PLURIBUS UNUM" will be full.

Extremely Fine (EF-40)

Obverse: All the major hair detail will show.

Reverse: All the major details of the feathers will show, but will be weak at the ends.

Note: The shield and eagle's wing or wings may be weak due to striking.

About Uncirculated (AU-50)

Obverse: Only a trace of wear will show on the shoulder and the highest waves of hair to the left of the ear and forehead.

Note: The obverse of this series, particularly 1806 and 1807, is struck more softly than other denominations of this period.

Reverse: Only a trace of wear will appear on the eagle's breast feathers and at the tips of the wings.

Large Capped Quarters
1815-1828

About Good (AG- 3)

Obverse: The rim will be worn down well into the stars.

Note: There may be partial "LIBERTY" lettering even in very low grades.

Reverse: The rim will be worn down well into the letters.

Good (G-4)

Obverse: The rim will be worn down to the tops of the stars.

Reverse: The rim may be worn down to the tops of some letters. The eagle's feathers and the banner on which "E PLURIBUS UNUM" appears will be worn smooth.

Very Good (VG-8)

Obverse: There will be a full rim. At least three full letters of "LIBERTY" must show.

Reverse: A partial "E PLURIBUS UNUM" will show.

Fine (F-12)

Obverse: "LIBERTY" will be complete and sharp. Half of the major hair detail will show. All the curls will be worn on the high points.

Reverse: There will be a full "E PLURIBUS UNUM" although a few letters may be weakly struck.

Large Capped Quarters
1815-1828

Very Fine (VF-20)

Obverse: The hair will be more detailed. Drapery will be well outlined.

Reverse: "E PLURIBUS UNUM" will be sharp. About two-thirds of the eagle's feathers will show.

Extremely Fine (EF-40)

Obverse: All the hair will be detailed but will show wear on the high points.

Reverse: All the feathers will be visible but the edges of the wings will show wear.

About Uncirculated (AU-50)

Obverse: Only a trace of wear will show on the hair above the eye and ear and the tips of the curls.

Note: May be weakly struck around the curl on the neck and the drapery clasp; grade of the coin cannot be determined by these features.

Reverse: There will be a slight trace of wear on the tips of the wings and the claws.

Small Capped Quarters
1831-1838

About Good (AG- 3)

Obverse: The rim will be worn down into the stars and/or date. The head will be worn smooth.

Reverse: The rim will be worn down into the letters. The eagle's feathers will be worn smooth.

Good (G-4)

Obverse: The stars and date will be full. There may be a partial "LIBERTY."

Reverse: The rim may be worn down to the tops of a few letters. A few feathers will begin to show.

Very Good (VG-8)

Obverse: There will be a full "LIBERTY" but a letter or two may be weak. Half of the major detail of the hair will show.

Reverse: The lettering will be bold. Half of the eagle's feathers will be visible.

Fine (F-12)

Obverse: "LIBERTY" will be strong. All the major hair detail will show but the curls will be worn flat.

Reverse: About three-quarters of the feathers will show but wear will be visible around the edges of the wings and on the neck.

Small Capped Quarters
1831-1838

Very Fine (VF-20)

Obverse: The hair curls will show less wear and appear more rounded.

Reverse: All the major details of the feathers will show. The leg, neck, and wings will show more detail.

Extremely Fine (EF-40)

Obverse: Wear will appear on the highest hair curls and the top of Liberty's cap.

Reverse: Wear will be visible on the high points of the feathers and claws.

About Uncirculated (AU-50)

Obverse: Only a trace of wear will show on the hair above the ear and around the forehead. The cheek will show slight wear.

Reverse: Only a trace of wear will show at the top and bottom tips of the wings and the eagle's left claw.

Liberty Seated Quarters
1838-1891

About Good (AG-3)

Obverse: The rim will be worn down into the date and/or stars.

Reverse: The rim will be worn down well into the lettering.

Good (G-4)

Obverse: There will be a full outline of the Liberty seated figure. The shield will be worn smooth.

Reverse: All lettering will be clear. The eagle will be worn smooth.

Very Good (VG-8)

Obverse: A total of any three letters (can be two full letters plus two half letters) of "LIBERTY" will be visible on the shield.

Reverse: The rim will be sharply defined. A few feathers will show on the eagle.

Fine (F-12)

Obverse: There will be a full "LIBERTY" on the shield but it will not be sharp.

Reverse: About half of the eagle's feathers will show.

Liberty Seated Quarters
1838-1891

Very Fine (VF-20)

Obverse: "LIBERTY" will be sharp. Only the deepest folds of Liberty's gown will be visible.

Reverse: Three-quarters of the feathers will be visible. Wear will show on the neck, leg, and edges of the wings.

Extremely Fine (EF-40)

Obverse: More detail on Liberty's gown will show. There will be wear on Liberty's head, breast, and legs.

Reverse: All the major details will be visible but will be worn on the high spots. The neck and claws will show slight wear.

About Uncirculated (AU-50)

Obverse: Only a trace of wear will appear on Liberty's breast and knees.

Note: The clasp of Liberty's gown may be weak due to striking and cannot be used to determine condition.

Reverse: Only a trace of wear will show on the neck, the claws, and the tops of the wings.

Note: Flat spots will sometimes occur due to striking.

Barber Quarters
1892-1916

About Good (AG-3)

Obverse: The rim will be worn down into the stars, letters, and/or date.

Reverse: The rim will be worn down into the lettering.

Good (G-4)

Obverse: The stars, letters, and date will be complete. The head will be well outlined but worn smooth.

Reverse: The rim may be worn down to the tops of a few letters. The eagle will be well outlined but worn smooth.

Very Good (VG-8)

Obverse: A total of any three letters (can be two full letters plus two half letters) of "LIBERTY" will show.

Reverse: A few feathers will show in the wings. A partial "E PLURIBUS UNUM" will show.

Fine (F-12)

Obverse: There will be a full "LIBERTY" on the head but it will not be sharp. The top of the wreath will be well outlined but the bottom will be worn.

Reverse: About half of the feathers will show. "E PLURIBUS UNUM" will be three-quarters complete.

Barber Quarters
1892-1916

Very Fine (VF-20)

Obverse: "LIBERTY" will be sharp. The wreath will be well outlined at both top and bottom.

Reverse: "E PLURIBUS UNUM" will be complete. More feather detail will show on the neck and tail.

Extremely Fine (EF-40)

Obverse: The edges of the band on which "LIBERTY" appears will be distinct. The wreath will be bold. There will be wear above the forehead.

Reverse: All the major detail of the feathers will show. Wear

will be apparent on the neck, tail, and upper edges of the wings.

About Uncirculated (AU-50)

Obverse: Only a trace of wear will appear on the hair above the forehead, the tips of the leaves in the wreath, and on the cheekbone.

Reverse: Only a trace of wear will be visible on the eagle's head, tail, and tips of the wings.

Liberty Standing Quarters
1916-1917

About Good (AG-3)

Obverse: The date will be identifiable although it will be barely visible.

Reverse: The rim will be worn down into the lettering and stars.

Good (G-4)

Obverse: The top portion of the date will be worn smooth. Date will be easily identified.

Reverse: All the lettering will be clear. The eagle will be outlined sharply but will be worn almost smooth.

Very Good (VG-8)

Obverse: The date will be complete but the very top will be weak. The band of cloth from Liberty's right hand to the shield will be outlined.

Reverse: One-third of the feathers will show.

Fine (F-12)

Obverse: The date will be sharp. The shield will be complete around its outer edge. Liberty's right leg will be worn flat.

Reverse: Half of the feathers will show.

Liberty Standing Quarters
1916-1917

Very Fine (VF-20)

Obverse: Liberty's right leg will be rounded but worn from above the gown to midway between the foot and knee. The gown line in the center of the upper leg will be worn.

Reverse: Almost all the major detail of the feathers will show. The eagle's body and the front edge of the right wing will be worn flat.

Extremely Fine (EF-40)

Obverse: Liberty's right leg will be worn on the knee. The gown line will be visible across the leg. The breast will be rounded.

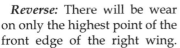

Reverse: There will be wear on only the highest point of the front edge of the right wing. Wear will be visible on the highest points of the eagle's body.

About Uncirculated (AU-50)

Obverse: Only a trace of wear will show on the knee cap, head, and center of the shield.

Reverse: Only a trace of wear will be seen on the highest point of the eagle's body.

Liberty Standing Quarters
1917-1924

About Good (AG-3)

Obverse: The date will be identifiable although barely visible.

Reverse: The rim may be worn down to the tops of some letters.

Note: The lower grades are basically determined by the date, so the reverses appear to be in better condition than on the quarters of 1925-1930.

Good (G-4)

Obverse: Wear will extend into the date but the date will be easily identified.

Note: The date was on a higher plane from 1917 to 1924. Grading from About Good to Fine should be determined by the wear on the date.

Reverse: The rim will be worn down to the tops of the letters.

Very Good (VG-8)

Obverse: The date will be complete but may be weak. The band of cloth from Liberty's right hand to the shield will be outlined on top.

Reverse: There will be a full rim. About one-third of the feathers will show.

Fine (F-12)

Obverse: The date will be sharp. The shield will be complete around its outer edge. Liberty's right leg will be worn flat.

Reverse: Approximately half of the feathers will show.

Liberty Standing Quarters
1917-1924

Very Fine (VF-20)

Obverse: Liberty's right leg will be rounded but worn from above the gown to the foot. About half of the mail covering the breast will show.

Reverse: The eagle's body will be worn smooth.

Extremely Fine (EF-40)

Obverse: Liberty's right knee and the tip of breast will show slight wear.

Reverse: All the feathers will show but will be worn on the high spots.

About Uncirculated (AU-50)

Obverse: Only a trace of wear will show on the knee cap, breast, and center of the shield.

Note: Usually struck with a flat head. An Uncirculated coin with a fully detailed head is worth a premium price.

Reverse: Only a trace of wear will show on the front edge of the eagle's wing and the high points of the breast.

Liberty Standing Quarters
1925-1930

About Good (AG-3)

Obverse: The rim will be worn down into the date and letters.

Reverse: The rim will be worn down into the lettering and stars.

Good (G-4)

Obverse: There will be a full date. The figure of Liberty will be worn smooth.

Reverse: The rim will be worn down to the tops of the letters.

Very Good (VG-8)

Obverse: More detail will appear in the folds of Liberty's gown and on her shield.

Reverse: There will be a full rim. About one-third of the feathers will show.

Fine (F-12)

Obverse: The shield will be complete around its outer edge. Liberty's right leg will be worn flat.

Reverse: Approximately half of the feathers will show.

Liberty Standing Quarters
1925-1930

Very Fine (VF-20)

Obverse: About half of the mail covering the breast will show.

Reverse: The eagle's body will be worn smooth.

Extremely Fine (EF-40)

Obverse: Liberty's right knee and the tip of her breast will show light wear.

Reverse: All the feathers will show but will be worn on the high spots.

About Uncirculated (AU-50)

Obverse: Only a trace of wear will show on Liberty's right knee and breast.

Note: Usually struck with a flat head.

Reverse: Only a trace of wear will show on the front edge of the eagle's wing and the high points of the breast.

Washington Quarters
1932 to Date

About Good (AG-3)

Obverse: The rim will be worn halfway into the letters and date.

Reverse: The rim will be worn halfway down into the letters.

Good (G-4)

Obverse: The rim will be worn into the tops of the letters and the bottom of the date.

Reverse: The rim will be worn down into the tops of the letters.

Very Good (VG-8)

Obverse: The rim will touch the tops of the letters and the bottom of the date.

Reverse: The rim will touch the tops of some of the letters.

Fine (F-12)

Obverse: There will be a full rim. The hairline will begin to show above the forehead.

Reverse: There will be a full rim. No feathers will show on the eagle's breast.

Washington Quarters
1932 to Date

Very Fine (VF-20)

Obverse: The major details of the hair will show but there will be considerable wear on the curls.

Note: The motto "IN GOD WE TRUST" is weakly struck on all 1932 and on some 1934 issues.

Reverse: Feathers will show on both sides of the eagle's breast.

Extremely Fine (EF-40)

Obverse: The hair on the highest points of the head and curls will show wear.

Reverse: There will be wear on the high points of the eagle's breast and legs.

About Uncirculated (AU-50)

Obverse: Only a trace of wear on the cheek, the high points of the hair, and around the ear.

Reverse: Only a trace of wear will be visible on the eagle's breast and tops of the legs.

Flowing Hair Half Dollars
1794-1795

About Good (AG-3)

Obverse: The rim will be worn down well into the design.

Reverse: The rim will be worn down well into the letters and design.

Good (G-4)

Obverse: The head will be well outlined but will show almost no detail. There may be a few weak spots around the rim.

Reverse: The rim may be worn down into the tops of some of the letters. The eagle will be outlined but will be worn completely smooth.

Very Good (VG-8)

Obverse: All the lettering and the date will be clear. About one-quarter of the hair detail will show.

Reverse: The breast of the eagle will be outlined against the wings.

Fine (F-12)

Obverse: About half of the detail will show in the hair. The top of the head will be worn smooth.

Reverse: Some feathers will show on eagle's left wing and tail.

Flowing Hair Half Dollars
1794-1795

Very Fine (VF-20)

Obverse: Approximately two-thirds of hair will show and will be outlined around the forehead.

Reverse: About half of the feathers will show. The leaves will be well defined.

Extremely Fine (EF-40)

Obverse: Almost all of the hair will show. The top of the head will still show a few wear spots.

Note: This series was generally softly struck, so the fine detail may not show—even on higher-grade specimens.

Reverse: Three-quarters of the feathers will show. The leaves will be well rounded but will be worn on the high points.

About Uncirculated (AU-50)

Obverse: All the hair will show. Only a slight trace of wear will show on the bust and highest waves of hair.

Reverse: A trace of wear will show on the top edges of the wings, breast, and head. The leaves will be well detailed.

Note: The breast feathers were usually weakly struck on this series.

Draped Bust Half Dollars
1796-1807
(For 1796-1797 reverses see
Draped Bust Dollars 1795-1804)

About Good (AG-3)

Obverse: The rim will be worn down into the letters, stars, and date.

Reverse: The rim will be worn down into the lettering and design.

Good (G-4)

Obverse: The letters, stars, and date will be clear. The head will be outlined but worn smooth.

Reverse: The lettering will be clear although the rim may be worn down to the tops of a few letters. The wings will be worn smooth.

Very Good (VG-8)

Obverse: About one-third of the hairlines will show.

Reverse: A partial "E PLURIBUS UNUM" will show. A few feathers will be visible.

Fine (F-12)

Obverse: More detail will show in the hair; the hair will be two-thirds complete.

Reverse: Approximately half of the eagle's feathers will show. At least half of "E PLURIBUS UNUM" will show.

Draped Bust Half Dollars
1796-1807
(For 1796-1797 reverses see
Draped Bust Dollars 1795-1804)

Very Fine (VF-20)

Obverse: About three-quarters of the hairlines will be visible.

Reverse: "E PLURIBUS UNUM" will be full. About three-quarters of the feathers will show.

Extremely Fine (EF-40)

Obverse: All the major hair details will show. There will be flatness due to wear above the forehead and on the back of the head.

Reverse: All the major details of the feathers will show. The ends and top edges of the wings will show wear.

About Uncirculated (AU-50)

Obverse: Only a trace of wear will show on the highest points of hair, cheek, and shoulder.

Reverse: Only a trace of wear will show on the top edges and tips of the wings, breast, head, and tail.

Capped Half Dollars
1807-1836

About Good (AG-3)

Obverse: The rim will be worn down into the stars and date.

Reverse: The rim will be worn down into the letters.

Good (G-4)

Obverse: The head will be outlined but will show no detail. There will be a partial "LIBERTY."

Reverse: All the letters will be complete. The eagle will be outlined but worn smooth.

Very Good (VG-8)

Obverse: A full "LIBERTY" will show. About half the major hair detail will be visible.

Reverse: A few feathers will be visible in the eagle's left wing.

Fine (F-12)

Obverse: About two-thirds of the major hair detail will show.

Reverse: Half of the feathers will show. The eagle's claws will be well outlined but show wear.

Capped Half Dollars
1807-1836

Very Fine (VF-20)

Obverse: All the major hair detail will show. The tops of the waves of hair will be worn flat.

Reverse: Nearly all the major details of the feathers will show. Definite wear will show on the high points of the feathers.

Extremely Fine (EF-40)

Obverse: The hair curls will be well rounded with wear only on the high points.

Note: The drapery clasp often is quite weak due to striking and should not be used to determine grade.

Reverse: All the feathers will
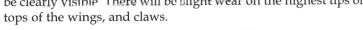
be clearly visible. There will be slight wear on the highest tips of the feathers, tops of the wings, and claws.

About Uncirculated (AU-50)

Obverse: Only a trace of wear will appear on the cheek, cap, and highest waves of hair above the forehead and ear.

Reverse: Only a trace of wear will show on the claws, the tops of the wings, and the head.

Note: Weak striking may obliterate part of "E PLURIBUS UNUM" and the upper right wing. This weakness should not alter the grade.

Reeded Edge Half Dollars
1836-1839

About Good (AG-3)

Obverse: The rim will be worn down well into the stars and date.

Reverse: The rim will be worn down well into the letters.

Good (G-4)

Obverse: The head will be outlined but worn almost completely smooth. There will be a partial "LIBERTY" showing.

Reverse: The eagle will be outlined but will show no feathers.

Note: The lettering on 1836 and 1837 halves will be weak due to a low rim. This must be taken into consideration when grading.

Very Good (VG-8)

Obverse: There will be a full "LIBERTY." A few waves of hair will show.

Reverse: A few feathers will be visible.

Fine (F-12)

Obverse: About half of the major hair details will show.

Reverse: Approximately half of the feathers will show.

Reeded Edge Half Dollars
1836-1839

Very Fine (VF-20)

Obverse: All the major hair detail will show but the tops of the waves of hair will be worn flat.

Reverse: Three-quarters of the feathers will show.

Extremely Fine (EF-40)

Obverse: The hair curls will be well rounded with wear only on the high points.

Reverse: All the feathers will be clearly visible but wear will show on the high points. The claws and the edges of the wings will show wear.

About Uncirculated (AU-50)

Obverse: Only a trace of wear will appear on the cheek, ear, cap, and hair above the forehead.

Reverse: Only a trace of wear will be visible on the highest edges of the wings, the head, and the claws.

Liberty Seated Half Dollars
1839-1891

About Good (AG-3)

Obverse: The rim will be worn down into the date and/or stars.

Reverse: The rim will be worn down well into the letters.

Good (G-4)

Obverse: There will be a full outline of the figure of Liberty. The shield will be worn smooth.

Reverse: The letters will be complete although the rim may be worn down to the tops of a few letters. The eagle will be worn smooth.

Very Good (VG-8)

Obverse: A total of any three letters (can be two full letters plus two half letters) of "LIBERTY" will be visible on the shield.

Reverse: The rim will be complete. A few feathers will show on the wings.

Fine (F-12)

Obverse: There will be a full "LIBERTY" on the shield, but it will not be sharp.

Reverse: About half of the eagle's feathers will show.

Liberty Seated Half Dollars
1839-1891

Very Fine (VF-20)

Obverse: "LIBERTY" will be sharp. Only the deepest folds of Liberty's gown will be visible.

Reverse: Nearly all the major details of the feathers will show. Definite wear will show on the high points of the feathers.

Extremely Fine (EF-40)

Obverse: More detail of Liberty's gown will show. There will be wear on Liberty's head, breast, and legs.

Reverse: All the feathers will be plainly visible. There will be slight wear on the highest tips of the feathers, the tops of the wings, and the claws.

About Uncirculated (AU-50)

Obverse: Only a trace of wear will appear on Liberty's breast and knees.

Note: The clasp of Liberty's gown may be weak due to striking, therefore it cannot be used to determine condition.

Reverse: Only a trace of wear will show on the head, claws, and tops of the wings.

Barber Half Dollars
1892-1915

About Good (AG-3)

Obverse: The rim will be worn down into the stars, letters, and/or date.

Reverse: The rim will be worn down into the lettering.

Good (G-4)

Obverse: The stars, letters, and date will be complete. The head will be well outlined but worn smooth.

Reverse: The rim may be worn down to the tops of a few letters. The eagle will be well defined but worn smooth.

Very Good (VG-8)

Obverse: A total of any three letters (can be two full letters plus two half letters) of "LIBERTY" will show.

Reverse: The rim will be complete. A few feathers and a partial "E PLURIBUS UNUM" will be visible.

Fine (F-12)

Obverse: There will be a full "LIBERTY" on the head, but it will not be sharp. The top of the wreath will be well outlined but the bottom will be worn.

Reverse: About half of the feathers will show. "E PLURIBUS UNUM" will be complete although a few letters may be weak.

Barber Half Dollars
1892-1915

Very Fine (VF-20)

Obverse: "LIBERTY" will be sharp. The wreath will be well outlined at both top and bottom.

Reverse: "E PLURIBUS UNUM" will be sharp. More feather detail will show on the neck and tail.

Extremely Fine (EF-40)

Obverse: The edges of the band on which "LIBERTY" is located will be distinct. The wreath will be bold. There will be wear above the forehead.

Reverse: All the major detail of the feathers will show. Wear will be apparent on the neck, tail, and upper edges of the wings.

About Uncirculated (AU-50)

Obverse: Only a trace of wear will appear on the hair above the forehead, on the tips of the leaves in the wreath, and on the cheek bone.

Reverse: Only a trace of wear will be visible on the head, tail, and tips of the wings.

Liberty Walking Half Dollars
1916-1947

About Good (AG-3)

Obverse: The rim will be worn down into the letters.

Reverse: The rim will be worn down into the letters.

Good (G-4)

Obverse: The rim will be worn to the tops of a few letters and the bottom of the date.

Reverse: The rim will be worn to the tops of the letters.

Very Good (VG-8)

Obverse: There will be a full rim. Half of the skirt lines will show (on 1921-1947 issues).

Note: From 1916 to 1920 the skirt lines are weak and cannot be used to determine grade.

Reverse: Full rim. A few feathers will show.

Liberty Walking Half Dollars
1916-1947

Fine (F-12)

Obverse: More detail will show in the skirt lines (1921-1947) and in the leaves on the left arm.

Reverse: Half of the feathers will show.

Very Fine (VF-20)

Obverse: All skirt lines will show (1921-1947). The body will be well rounded and the breast will be outlined.

Reverse: All wing feathers will show. Breast will be worn smooth.

Extremely Fine (EF-40)

Obverse: There will be light wear on the head, breast, and left leg.

Reverse: High point of breast and left leg will be worn.

Liberty Walking Half Dollars
1916-1947

About Uncirculated (AU-50)

Obverse: Only a trace of wear will show on the highest points of the head, breast, and left arm.

Reverse: A trace of wear will show on the breast, leg, and wing tip.

Franklin Half Dollars
1948-1963

Good (G-4)

Obverse: The rim will be worn down into the lettering.

Reverse: The rim will be worn down into the lettering.

Very Good (VG-8)

Obverse: There will be a full rim. Hair behind the ear will be worn smooth.

Reverse: The rim will be worn down to the tops of the letters.

Fine (F-12)

Obverse: Some hair detail will show behind the ear. The cheek will be worn flat.

Reverse: There will be a full rim.

Very Fine (VF-20)

Obverse: All the major hairlines will show. The cheek will show wear but will be well rounded.

Reverse: About half of the horizontal lines on the bell will show.

Franklin Half Dollars
1948-1963

Extremely Fine (EF-40)

Obverse: More hair detail will show.

Reverse: Two-thirds of the horizontal lines will show wear.

About Uncirculated (AU-50)

Obverse: Only a trace of wear will be visible on the cheek, shoulder, and hair to the left of the ear.

Reverse: Only a trace of wear will show on the top of the bell and on the horizontal lines.

Kennedy Half Dollars
1964 to Date

Extremely Fine (EF-40)

Obverse: Wear will appear on the cheek and highest portion of hair to the right of the forehead.

Reverse: The head, shield, tail, and top edges of the wings will show wear.

About Uncirculated (AU-50)

Obverse: Only a trace of wear will show on the cheek and highest portion of the hair.

Reverse: Just a trace of wear will appear on the neck and highest point of the tail.

Flowing Hair Dollars
1794-1795

About Good (AG-3)

Obverse: The rim will be worn down into the stars, legend, and/or date.

Reverse: The rim will be worn down into the lettering.

Good (G-4)

Obverse: Liberty's head will be outlined but show no details. The stars, legend, and date will be clearly readable.

Reverse: The rim will be worn down to the tops of some of the lettering. The eagle will be worn smooth.

Very Good (VG-8)

Obverse: Major facial details will be visible. The bottom strands of hair will show.

Reverse: The eagle's outline and the feathers around the body will be visible. The wings will be worn smooth.

Fine (F-12)

Obverse: Approximately half of the major hair detail will show.

Reverse: The major feather details will show in the eagle's right wing.

Flowing Hair Dollars
1794-1795

Very Fine (VF-20)

Obverse: Two-thirds of the hair detail will show.

Reverse: Approximately half of the feather detail will show.

Extremely Fine (EF-45)

Obverse: All the major hair detail will be visible. The hair around the face and forehead will show wear.

Reverse: All the major feather detail will be visible on the wings and tail. The breast will be smooth. The wing tips and edges will show wear.

About Uncirculated (AU-50)

Obverse: Only a trace of wear will show on the tips of the highest curls and on the hair to the left of the forehead.

Reverse: Only a trace of wear will show on the head, breast, and tops of the wings.

Note: The breast feathers were usually weakly struck on this series. Many 1794 dollars are weakly struck at the lower left obverse and the corresponding part of the reverse. The hair detail is flatly struck on certain 1795 dollars.

Draped Bust Dollars
1795-1804

About Good (AG-3)
Obverse: The rim will be worn down into the stars, legend, and/or date.

Reverse: The rim will be worn down into the letters.

Good (G-4)
Obverse: The head will be boldly outlined. There will be a full rim.

Reverse: All letters will be readable.

Very Good (VG-8)
Obverse: The bottom and top curls will show some detail. The rest of the hair will be worn smooth.

Reverse. Full rim, with partial "E PLURIBUS UNUM" (on large eagle).

Draped Bust Dollars
1795-1804

Fine (F-12)

Obverse: Approximately half of the hair detail will show.

Note: Drapery line details vary too much from one variety to another to be accurately used to determine grade.

Reverse: Half of the feathers will show. "E PLURIBUS UNUM" will be weak.

Very Fine (VF-20)

Obverse: Two-thirds of the hair detail will show.

Reverse: Three-quarters of the feathers will show.

Extremely Fine (EF-40)

Obverse: All major hair detail will show. The highest waves of hair to the left of the neck and forehead will be worn.

Reverse: Slight wear on the breast and top edges of the wings.

Draped Bust Dollars
1795-1804

About Uncirculated (AU-50)

Obverse: Only a trace of wear will show on the bust, shoulder, and the hair left of the forehead.

Reverse: Traces of wear will show on the breast and extreme top edges of the wings.

Liberty Seated Dollars
1840-1873

About Good (AG-3)

Obverse: The rim will be worn down into the date and/or stars.

Reverse: The rim will be worn down well into the letters.

Good (G-4)

Obverse: There will be a full rim. The figure of Liberty will be sharply outlined. The shield will be worn smooth.

Reverse: The letters will be complete although the rim may be worn down to the tops of a few letters. The eagle will be worn smooth.

Very Good (VG-8)

Obverse: A total of any three letters (can be two full letters plus two half letters) of "LIBERTY" will show on the shield. A few major gown lines will show.

Reverse: Rim will be complete. A few feathers will show on the wings.

Fine (F-12)

Obverse: The "LI" and "TY" of "LIBERTY" will be clearly visible but only the top of "BER" will show.

Note: The shield is raised higher on this series and thus shows wear more quickly than on the Liberty

Seated dime, quarter, or half dollar. Different grading standards must be used.

Reverse: About half of the eagle's feathers will show high points of the feathers.

Liberty Seated Dollars
1840-1873

Very Fine (VF-20)

Obverse: "LIBERTY" will be complete with weakness showing only at the bottom part of "BE." All the major gown lines will show.

Reverse: Nearly all the major details of the feathers will show. Definite wear will show on the high points of the feathers.

Extremely Fine (EF-40)

Obverse: "LIBERTY" will be sharp. The breast will be outlined but worn on the high points. The head and Liberty's right leg will show wear.

Reverse: All the feathers will be plainly visible. There will be slight wear on the highest tips of the feathers, the tops of the wings, and the claws.

About Uncirculated (AU-50)

Obverse: Only a trace of wear will show on the head, knee, and tips of the breasts.

Reverse: Only a trace of wear will show on the claws, head, and the tops of the wings.

Morgan Dollars
1878-1921

Good (G-4)

Obverse: The hair above the forehead and ear will be worn smooth.

Reverse: The rim will be worn down to the tops of the letters.

Very Good (VG-8)

Obverse: The deepest strands of hair will be visible above the forehead. The hair above the ear will be worn smooth.

Reverse: Approximately one-third of the feathers will show on the eagle. The head and breast will be worn smooth.

Fine (F-12)

Obverse: Approximately half of the hairlines will show from the top of the head to the ear.

Reverse: Three-quarters of the major feather detail will show on the wings. The breast will be worn smooth.

Very Fine (VF-20)

Obverse: Three-quarters of the hairlines will show. The high points of the bottom curls will show considerable wear.

Reverse: All the feathers will show on the wings. There will be wear on the center breast feathers and the top edges of the wings.

Morgan Dollars
1878-1921

Extremely Fine (EF-40)

Obverse: All the hairlines will show. Wear will appear on the high points around the ear.

Reverse: There will be wear on the head and the highest points of the breast feathers.

About Uncirculated (AU-50)

Obverse: Only a trace of wear will show on the hair just above the ear and on the high points of hair above the forehead.

Reverse: Only a trace of wear will show on the highest points of the breast and head.

Note: Certain issues, particularly those of the branch mints, often come weakly struck on the eagle's breast, and allowances must be made for this in these instances.

Peace Dollars
1921-1935

Very Good (VG-8)

Obverse: The head will be worn smooth.

Note: This coin rarely is found in grades below Very Good.

Reverse: The word "PEACE" will show although a few letters may be weak.

Fine (F-12)

Obverse: The high waves of hair above the forehead and ear will be worn flat.

Reverse: The right wing will be outlined but only a few feathers will show.

Very Fine (VF-20)

Obverse: The hair above the forehead will be worn.

Note: The word "GOD" was often weakly struck. This does not affect the grade.

Reverse: The major details will show. Considerable wear will cause flatness on the right wing and head.

Extremely Fine (EF-40)

Obverse: All the hairlines will show. There will be some flatness on the highest waves of hair from wear.

Note: 1921 issues are in higher relief and often are found with weakly struck hair, even on top-grade examples.

Reverse: All the feathers will show, but not distinctly.

Peace Dollars
1921-1935

About Uncirculated (AU-50)

Obverse: Only a trace of wear will show on Liberty's cheek and the highest waves of her hair above the forehead and ear.

Reverse: Only a trace of wear will show on the neck and the top outside edge of the right wing.

Eisenhower Dollars
1971-1978

Very Fine (VF-20)

Obverse: There will be considerable wear on the cheek and jaw bones. Wear will also show on the neck and top of the head.

Reverse: There will be wear on the eagle's breast, left leg, and top feathers of the wings.

Extremely Fine (EF-40)

Obverse: Slight wear will show on the cheek and jaw bones, and the top of the head.

Reverse: There will be slight wear on the eagle's breast, left leg, and tops of the wings.

About Uncirculated (AU-50)

Obverse: Only a trace of wear will show on the cheek and jaw bones, and the top of the head.

Reverse: Only a trace of wear will appear on the eagle's breast, left leg, and top of the left wing.

Trade Dollars
1873-1885

Good (G-4)

Obverse: The figure of Liberty will be well outlined but will be worn smooth.

Reverse: Motto "E PLURIBUS UNUM" above the eagle will be worn away.

Very Good (VG-8)

Obverse: A partial "IN GOD WE TRUST" will show above the date. A few gown lines will show.

Reverse: A partial "E PLURIBUS UNUM" will show. About one-third of the feathers will be visible.

Fine (F-12)

Obverse: "IN GOD WE TRUST" will be complete but will show weakness at the top. "LIBERTY" will also be complete although weak.

Reverse: Motto "E PLURIBUS UNUM" will show although a few letters will be weak. Half of the feathers will be visible.

Very Fine (VF-20)

Obverse: "IN GOD WE TRUST" and "LIBERTY" will be strong. The major details of the gown will be visible.

Reverse: There will be a strong "E PLURIBUS UNUM" but it will show definite wear. Three-quarters of the feathers will be visible.

Trade Dollars
1873-1885

Extremely Fine (EF-40)

Obverse: All the gown lines will show, especially in Liberty's lap. There will be wear on the head, breast, and left leg.

Reverse: All the feathers will be visible. Wear will show on the head, knee, and outer edges of the wings.

About Uncirculated (AU-50)

Obverse: Only a trace of wear will appear on Liberty's left knee, tip of her left breast, and the hair above her ear.

Reverse: Only a trace of wear will show on the head, knee, and tops of the wings.

Gold Dollars Type I
1849-1854

Fine (F-12)

Obverse: A full "LIBERTY" will be visible. The hair will be worn smooth all along the forehead and above the ear.

Reverse: The individual leaves will be well defined but the fine details will not show.

Very Fine (VF-20)

Obverse: The hair will be outlined above the forehead and around the neck.

Reverse: Some fine details will begin to show in the centers of the leaves.

Extremely Fine (EF-40)

Obverse: All the major hair detail will show. Wear will be visible only on the highest waves of hair.

Reverse: All the leaves will show fine center detail. Wear will be visible on the tips of the leaves.

About Uncirculated (AU-50)

Obverse: Only a trace of wear will appear on the tips of the curls above the forehead and ear.

Note: Gold coins (of all denominations) are rarely found in grades below Fine.

Reverse: Only a trace of wear will show on the tips of the leaves.

Gold Dollars Type II
1854-1856

Fine (F-12)
Obverse: The hair will be worn smooth above the forehead and ear. Some of the feathers will be worn almost smooth.

Reverse: The wreath will be boldly outlined but will show only major detail.

Very Fine (VF-20)
Obverse: The hair will be outlined above the forehead and around the ear.

Reverse: Some of the fine leaf detail will begin to show.

Extremely Fine (EF-40)
Obverse: All the major hair detail will show.

Note: "LIBERTY" was often weakly struck on this series.

Reverse: There will be wear on all the high points of the wreath.

About Uncirculated (AU-50)
Obverse: Just a trace of wear will show on the hair above the forehead.

Reverse: Only a trace of wear will appear on the tips of the leaves.

Note: The two center figures of the date often show severe weakness due to striking and should not affect the grade of the coin.

Gold Dollars Type III
1856-1889

Fine (F-12)

Obverse: The hair above the forehead and ear will be worn smooth. The tops of the feathers will be smooth.

Reverse: The wreath will be boldly outlined but will show only major detail.

Very Fine (VF-20)

Obverse: The tops of the feathers and the hair around the face will be well outlined.

Reverse: Some of the fine leaf detail will begin to show.

Extremely Fine (EF-40)

Obverse: All the major hair detail will show. Only a slight amount of wear will be visible on the tips of the feathers.

Reverse: Wear will be visible on only the high points of the wreath.

About Uncirculated (AU-50)

Obverse: Traces of wear will show only on the tips of the feathers and on the hair above the ear and forehead.

Reverse: Just slight traces of wear will show on the tips of the leaves.

Capped Quarter Eagles
1796-1807

Fine (F-12)

Obverse: Liberty's cap will be worn almost smooth. Only the deepest waves of hair will show.

Reverse: Only the deepest lines in the feathers will show. "E PLURIBUS UNUM" will not be sharp, although it will be readable.

Very Fine (VF-20)

Obverse: The major detail of Liberty's cap will show. More hair detail will be visible.

Reverse: Most of the feathers will show but will be worn on the ends. "E PLURIBUS UNUM" will be sharp. The tail will show wear.

Note. "E PLURIBUS UNUM" may be weak in the center due to striking.

Extremely Fine (EF-40)

Obverse: There will be wear on the tops of the curls by Liberty's neck and on the highest folds of her cap.

Note: There may be weakness due to striking in the center of the obverse.

Reverse: Wear will be visible on the head, tail, and upper edges and tips of the wings.

About Uncirculated (AU-50)

Obverse: Only a trace of wear will be visible on the very top of the highest curls by Liberty's neck. A trace of wear will also be visible on the highest fold of her cap.

Reverse: Only a trace of wear will show on the tip of the head and the extreme upper edges of the wings.

Bust Quarter Eagles
1808-1839

Fine (F-12)

Obverse: The hair above the forehead will be worn smooth. Only the deepest curls of the hair will show.

Reverse: About half of the eagle's feathers will show. The neck will be worn smooth.

Very Fine (VF-20)

Obverse: "LIBERTY" will be very bold. All the major hair detail will show.

Reverse: Considerable wear will show on the head, neck, and edges and tips of the wings.

Extremely Fine (EF-40)

Obverse: Wear will be visible on the high points of the hair or cap above "LIBERTY" and on the curls around the neck.

Reverse: Wear will be visible on the head, neck, and upper edges of the wings.

Note: Weakness due to striking may appear on the eagle's right wing.

About Uncirculated (AU-50)

Obverse: Only a trace of wear will show on the very highest tips of the hair and cap.

Note: The same hair rules for grading should be used for the three minor types in this series.

Reverse: Only a trace of wear will appear on the highest point of the upper edges of the wings and highest feathers on the neck.

Liberty Head Quarter Eagles
1840-1907

Fine (F-12)

Obverse: "LIBERTY" will be complete but the "L" and "Y" may be weak. The hair curl on the neck, although outlined, will not show detail.

Reverse: About half of the feathers will show on the wings. The neck will be worn almost smooth.

Very Fine (VF-20)

Obverse: "LIBERTY" will be bold. The major hair detail will show.

Reverse: Three-quarters of the feathers will show.

Extremely Fine (EF-40)

Obverse: Wear will appear on the tops of the waves of hair above the forehead and ear and on top of the head.

Reverse: All the feathers will show, but there will be wear on the end of each feather.

About Uncirculated (AU-50)

Obverse: There will be only a trace of wear on the hair above the ear and forehead.

Reverse: Only a trace of wear will be visible on the head just below the eagle's eye, the tips of the wings, and on the eagle's left claw.

Indian Head Quarter Eagles
1908-1929

Very Fine (VF-20)

Obverse: The design on the band just above the forehead will be well worn and show only partial detail.

Reverse: The neck and upper end of the wing will be worn smooth. The feathers in the top half of the wing and breast will show wear.

Extremely fine (EF-40)

Obverse: The design on the band just above the forehead will be complete. Wear will be visible on the cheek, the feathers behind the ear, and the row of small feathers on top of the head.

Reverse: Wear will show on the neck, breast, and tip of the wing.

About Uncirculated (AU-50)

Obverse: Only a trace of wear will show on the cheek. The small row of feathers will show wear on the tips.

Reverse: Only a trace of wear will be visible on the upper neck and on the tops of the feathers at the tip of the wing.

Three-Dollar Gold
1854-1889

Fine (F-12)

Obverse: The hair above the forehead will be worn into the bottom of the first few letters of "LIBERTY." The tops of the feathers will be worn smooth.

Reverse: The wreath will be boldly outlined but show only major detail.

Very Fine (VF-20)

Obverse: The tops of the feathers will be well outlined but will show little detail. The hair above the forehead will touch "LI" of "LIBERTY."

Reverse: Some of the fine leaf detail will begin to show.

Extremely Fine (EF-40)

Obverse: The hair above the forehead will be outlined but worn on the high point. All major details will show in the hair and on the feathers.

Reverse: There will be wear on all the high points of the wreath.

Note: The date may be weak due to striking.

About Uncirculated (AU-50)

Obverse: A trace of wear will appear on the hair above the forehead and ear and on the tips of the feathers.

Note: The hair curls by the neck often come weakly struck and cannot be used to determine condition.

Reverse: Only a trace of wear will show on the ends of the leaves and the ribbon knot.

Capped Half Eagles
1795-1807
(For Small Eagle reverse see
Capped Eagles 1795-1804)

Very Fine (VF-20)

Obverse: The hair, cap, and bust will show wear on the high points.

Reverse: Most of the feathers will show although they will be worn on the ends. The tail will show wear.

Extremely Fine (EF-40)

Obverse: Wear will be visible on the highest points of the cap, the hair above the forehead and to the left of the ear.

Reverse: Wear will be visible on the head, tail, and upper edges and tips of the wings.

Note: "E PLURIBUS UNUM" may be weak in the center due to striking.

About Uncirculated (AU-50)

Obverse: Traces of wear will show only on the highest waves of hair above the forehead and behind the ear.

Note: The hair by the neck may be weakly struck.

Reverse: A trace of wear will show only on the extreme upper edges of the wings and the tip of the head.

Bust Half Eagles
1807-1838

Very Fine (VF-20)

Obverse: "LIBERTY" will be very bold. All major details of the hair will show.

Reverse: Considerable wear will show on the head, neck, and ends of the wings.

Extremely Fine (EF-40)

Obverse: Wear will be visible on the high points of the hair or cap above "LIBERTY" and on the lower hair curls.

Reverse: Wear will be visible on the head, neck, and upper edges of the wings.

About Uncirculated (AU-50)

Obverse: A trace of wear will show only on the very highest tips of the hair and cap.

Note: The same basic rules for grading should be used for the three minor types in this series.

Reverse: Only a trace of wear

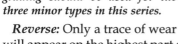

will appear on the highest part of the upper edge of the wings and the highest feathers on the neck.

Liberty Head Half Eagles
1839-1908

Fine (F-12)

Obverse: "LIBERTY" will be complete although the "L" may be weak. The hair will show considerable wear.

Reverse: About half of the feathers will show on the wings. The neck will be worn almost smooth.

Very Fine (VF-20)

Obverse: "LIBERTY" will be bold. The major hair detail will show.

Reverse: Three-quarters of the feathers will show. More detail will appear on the eagle's right leg.

Extremely Fine (EF-40)

Obverse: Wear will appear on the tops of the waves of hair above the ear and forehead and on top of the head.

Reverse: All the feathers will show but there will be wear on the end of each feather.

About Uncirculated (AU-50)

Obverse: There will be only a trace of wear on the hair above the ear and forehead.

Reverse: Only a trace of wear will be visible on the head just below the eagle's eye, the tips of the wings, and on the eagle's left claw.

Indian Head Half Eagles
1908-1929

Very fine (VF-20)

Obverse: The design on the band above the forehead will be well worn and will show only partial detail.

Reverse: The neck and upper end of the wing will be worn smooth.

Extremely Fine (EF-40)

Obverse: The design on the band just above the forehead will be complete. Wear will be visible on the cheek, the feathers behind the ear, and the row of small feathers on top of the head.

Reverse: Wear will show on the neck, breast, and tip of the wing.

About Uncirculated (AU-50)

Obverse: Only a trace of wear will show on the cheek. The small row of feathers will show wear on their tips.

Reverse: Only a trace of wear will be visible on the upper neck and on the tops of the feathers at the tip of the wing.

Capped Eagles
1795-1804

Very Fine (VF-20)

Obverse: The hair, cap, and bust will show wear on the high points.

Reverse: Most feathers will be visible but will be worn on the ends.

Extremely Fine (EF-40)

Obverse: Wear will be visible on the highest points of the cap and on the hair above the forehead and to the left of the ear.

Reverse: Wear will be on the head, breast, and upper edges and tips of the wings.

About Uncirculated (AU-50)

Obverse: Only traces of wear will show on the highest waves of hair above the forehead and behind the ear.

Reverse: Traces of wear on extreme edges of the wings, tip of the head, and breast.

Liberty Head Eagles
1838-1907

Fine (F-12)

Obverse: "LIBERTY" will be complete but the "L" may be weak. The hair will show considerable wear.

Reverse: About half of the feathers will show on the wings. The neck will be worn almost smooth.

Very Fine (VF-20)

Obverse: "LIBERTY" will be bold. The major hair detail will show.

Reverse: About three-quarters of the feathers will show.

Extremely Fine (EF-40)

Obverse: Wear will appear on the top of the waves of hair above the forehead and ear and on top of the head.

Reverse: All the feathers will show but there will be wear on the end of each feather.

About Uncirculated (AU-50)

Obverse: There will be only a trace of wear on the hair above the ear and forehead.

Reverse: Only a trace of wear will be visible on the head just below the eagle's eye and on the tips and extreme upper edges of the wings.

Indian Head Eagles
1907-1933

Very Fine (VF-20)

Obverse: Considerable wear will show on the feathers just above the word "LIBERTY" and on the hair above the ear and forehead.

Reverse: Three-quarters of the eagle's feathers will show. Wear will be visible on the head, top of the left wing, and on the high points of the legs.

Extremely Fine (EF-40)

Obverse: Slight wear will show on the hair and feathers just above the word "LIBERTY."

Reverse: Less wear will show on the left wing, head, and legs.

About Uncirculated (AU-50)

Obverse: There will be a trace of wear on the highest waves of hair above the ear and eye.

Reverse: Only a trace of wear will be visible on the tip of the left wing and tip of the head.

Liberty Head Double Eagles
1849-1907

Fine (F-12)

Obverse: The hair on top of the head and below the coronet will be worn smooth. The curls by the neck will show only major details.

Reverse: The eagle's head will be worn smooth. The tail and the tops of the wings will show considerable wear.

Very Fine (VF-20)

Obverse: The major hair detail will show on top of the head and below the coronet.

Reverse: All the feathers will show on the wings but they will not be sharply detailed.

Extremely Fine (EF-40)

Obverse: Wear will show on the curls by the neck and on the hair above the ear and below the coronet.

Note: The hair curl directly under the ear will sometimes be weak due to striking. Carson City issues usually lack the detail of coins from other mints.

Reverse: The feathers on the wings will be sharp. Wear will be visible on the head, neck, tail, and the highest points of the shield.

About Uncirculated (AU-50)

Obverse: Only a trace of wear will be visible on the highest waves of hair.

Reverse: The slightest trace of wear will show on the eagle's neck and the tip of the tail.

Note: "E PLURIBUS UNUM" will not always be fully readable, even on Uncirculated coins, due to striking.

Saint-Gaudens Double Eagles
1907-1933

Fine (F-12)

Obverse: Liberty's right leg will be worn almost smooth. The gown line across the chest will be weak.

Reverse: The forward edge of the left wing will show wear. The breast and leg will show smooth spots of wear.

Very Fine (VF-20)

Obverse: More detail will be visible in Liberty's gown around the breasts and on her lower right leg.

Reverse: Just the tip of the left wing will show wear. The breast will show a smooth spot

of wear. Wear will be visible on the leg but the feathers will be discernible.

Extremely Fine (EF-40)

Obverse: There will be wear on the breasts and both knees.

Reverse: All the feathers will show except a small spot on the breast just behind the neck.

Note: Light bag marks are to be expected on most issues; heavy bag marks or dents will lower the value of scarcer pieces.

About Uncirculated (AU-50)

Obverse: Only a trace of wear will show on the tips of the breasts and Liberty's left knee.

Note: A flat knee and/or nose may appear on Uncirculated coins due to coin-to-coin contact in the mint or banks.

Reverse: The slightest trace of wear will be noticeable on the breast, just behind the neck.

Colonial and Early American Coins

I have separated the various styles and qualities of strikes among colonial coins into three basic groups.

The Connecticut copper coins pictured on this page represent the first group. These crudely struck pieces were made from handcrafted dies. Interesting, sometimes comical, die cutting errors abound in the Connecticut series, as do off center strikes, incomplete or very weak design portions (due to striking, not to wear), and misaligned dies. Planchet imperfections are also quite common among Connecticut cents. Generally, the issues of 1785, the first year of Connecticut coinage, are the best from the standpoint of sharp striking. 1786 and 1787 issues are in lower relief and are less carefully struck. 1788 issues, the last year, are nearly always poorly and shallowly struck. Sometimes Connecticut cents, particularly issues of 1788, are found over struck on other colonial and related issues such as Nova Constellatio coppers and Irish halfpennies. All these aspects contribute to the romance of Connecticut issues. Specialists find Connecticut cents to be fascinating. They eagerly search, because over 300 die varieties are known to exist.

Other popular colonials in this first group include all Massachusetts silver issues, Mark Newby pieces, Nova Eborac coppers, the Auctori Plebis token, Voce Populi coppers, and copper coins of Vermont. Like Connecticut coins, these issues were all made from handcrafted, often crude (by later standards) dies.

Colonial and Early American Coins

Good	VG	Fine	VF

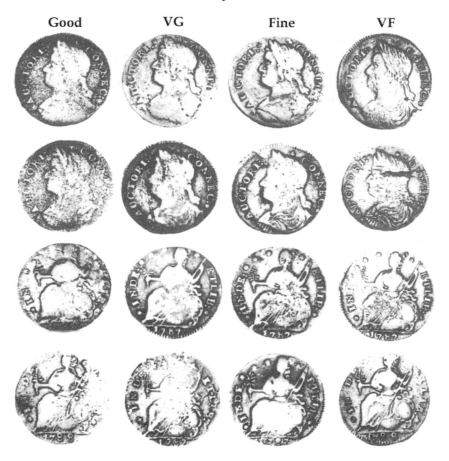

Colonial and Early American Coins

The second group of representative colonial coins contains coins that were originally struck with more care and precision than the first group. Included in the second group are New Jersey coppers (as illustrated here), Maryland silver issues, Rosa Americana coinage, Wood's or Hibernia pieces of 1722-1724, New York issues (except Nova Eborac and certain Machin's issues), Massachusetts cents and half cents of 1787 and 1788, Continental dollars, Nova Constellatio coppers, French colonies issues, Chalmers' silver coinage, Elephant tokens, Virginia halfpennies, North American tokens, Pitt tokens, Washington pieces of United States origin, and Fugio cents.

Of these series, the Massachusetts copper coins were struck with the most uniformity. Well-centered and well-struck pieces are the rule, not the exception. Likewise, Hibernia and Virginia issues, both of which were made in England, are usually found well struck. Elephant tokens vary: some are well struck; others show weakness in portions. Nova Constellatio coppers and Continental dollars are usually well struck, and well centered. Rosa Americana pieces, while well made, are apt to have a porous surface due to the nature of the alloy, called "bath metal", used for most of these pieces. Fugio cent dies were well made and are quite uniform in general appearance. Striking varied from time to time. Some show weakness, especially on the center of the obverse.

New Jersey coppers, (illustrated here) were generally well struck. However, there were exceptions. With over 100 known die varieties, many, especially some of the rarer ones, are found with indistinct design portions.

Colonial and Early American Coins

Good	VG	Fine	VF

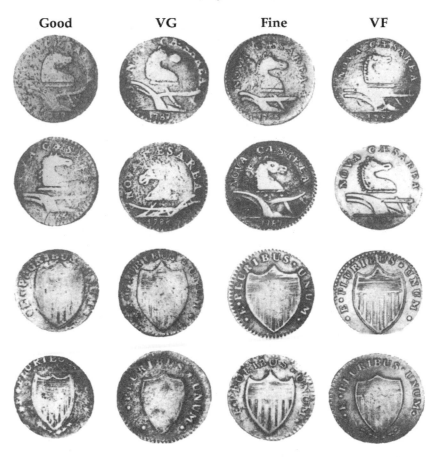

Colonial and Early American Coins

The third group of coins comprises well-struck issues, mostly of English origin. In England the state of the minting art, or at least the state of minting practice, was well advanced over that used in the United States during the c.1780-1820 period. During this period most coins in this third group were struck.

Illustrated on this page are Washington pieces of English origin, which serve to illustrate this group. Also in this group are the Bar cents, Kentucky tokens, Myddelton tokens, Franklin Press tokens, and the Rhode Island Ship tokens. Most third-group coins are in Very Good or better grades when found today. Unlike most group-one and group-two colonials, many of the group-three coins are known in Uncirculated grade.

There are idiosyncrasies, to be sure, among coins of the third group. UNITY STATES "cents" are invariably found on striated planchets, with weak obverse lettering. 1793 Ship halfpennies usually display a die bulge at the lower right portion of the reverse. Still other issues (the Myddelton tokens and 1791 large and small-eagle cents are examples) perfectly struck and with excellent design detail are nearly always found .

Note: In recent years a number of forgeries of the 1776 Continental dollar, Bar cent, and many other colonial issues have been made ostensibly for "souvenir" purposes. Occasionally these pieces, usually crude in appearance, find their way into numismatic channels. Most have a porous and pebbly surface and fail the "ring test" (see Counterfeit coin section). As is true when buying any rare or expensive coin, your best protection is to buy from an established professional dealer who guarantees what he sells.

Colonial and Early American Coins

VG	Fine	VF	EF

Chapter 7

The Minting Procedure

Knowledge of the minting procedure is a useful adjunct to grading. As strange as it may seem to the uninitiated, even before a coin leaves the mint it can show extensive signs of handling! The next several paragraphs provide useful information about the study of Uncirculated grades, from MS-60 to MS-70. Then follows a general discussion of historical minting procedures.

A Coining Factory

The primary purpose of a mint is to produce coins for the channels of commerce. Literally, a mint is a coining factory. Operated by the government, the Philadelphia Mint, for example, has as its challenge the production of the greatest amount of coins in the quickest amount of time at the lowest cost to taxpayers. While mints sometimes produce pieces just for collectors (especially Proof coins, medals, etc.), their everyday job is churning out cascades of cents, nickels, dimes, and other coins to serve in financial transactions.

Today, coin production is highly mechanized. Pieces are not carefully scrutinized by human eyes or touched by human hands. The experience of a Lincoln cent at the Philadelphia Mint is typical. Such a process was seen by the writer in 1979:

(1) Our cent begins as a strip of copper alloy. Fed through a press, the strip is cut out by a series of round punches, just like cookies are cut out of a strip of dough. A coppery stream of planchets cascades into a bin. One hundred thousand or more pieces can be produced in an hour by the device.

(2) Next, the planchets are run through a sieve-like machine which serves to extract pieces which are notably undersized or oversized. By this point, the typical planchet has been jiggled and jostled against many others and displays a profusion of tiny nicks, scratches, and other marks.

(3) Next comes the upsetting machine. A planchet runs through this device, which by means of a roller squeezes it to a slightly smaller diameter, raising a rim around the obverse and reverse. Before and after this process the planchet is again shuffled with many others of its kind.

(4) The planchets then go through a bath and are washed to remove foreign material, grease, loose particles, etc. from the surface. This is done in mass, with the pieces continuing to jostle against each other.

(5) The typical planchet is now ready for coining. Transferred in a metal bin, the planchets are dumped into a hopper which feeds into an automatic press. The press contains multiple dies, so that two or four pieces can be struck in a single blow. At this point our typical coin is "born." Struck at lightning speed, it is mechanically ejected from the dies. At this very instant, it begins to acquire marks, from the ejection mechanism. However, if the presses were stopped, and the piece extracted from the dies by a gloved hand, at this point in time, and at this point only, we would have a piece in perfect grade, or MS-70 preservation. Still, it might show some planchet marks, or nicks remaining from the planchet state, and not obliterated by striking pressure.

(6) The cent is then ejected into a metal chute, where it slides along with other cents and is dumped into a metal receiving bin, after which thousands of other cents are dumped on top of it.

(7) At periodic intervals the receiving bin is taken away, mechanically lifted, and its contents are poured into a large metal cart. By this time the freshly minted Lincoln cent has been slid, rubbed, and jostled against many others and, if examined, would be lucky to be in the grade known as MS-65 by collectors! But, this is not all.

(8) Finished coins are then removed to another section of the mint, where they are dumped into a hopper, fed through a chute, and spun through a high-speed mechanical counting device, at the end of which is a spout through which cents pour into a cloth bag. After 5,000 cents ($50 face value) worth of cents have been counted, the cascade stops, the bag is removed, and is sealed.

(9) The bag is then thrown on a cart, where it remains as other cloth bags full of cents are heaped upon it. After many bags are loaded on the cart, the coins are transferred to a storage vault, where they remain until they are called for by various banks in the Federal Reserve system. During this stay, or during their later stay at a Federal Reserve bank, no effort is made to prevent the pieces from becoming moist, or subjected to fumes, or to prevent further handling.

(10) Our typical cent, immersed in a bag with 4,999 others is called for by a Federal Reserve bank. It is loaded on the bed of a truck, other bags are thrown on top of it, and off the shipment goes to the Federal Reserve bank placing the order, possibly hundreds of miles distant. As the truck stops and starts, goes over roads, and negotiates turns, the coins in each bag slip and slide further.

(11) At the Federal Reserve bank, the sacks of coins are off-loaded and put into storage vaults, again being tossed and stacked, and again causing each cent to acquire more surface marks.

(12) A commercial bank orders coins from the Federal Reserve, and our typical cent is shipped in its cloth bag to its final banking destination, which involves another trip by truck, more jostling and movement, and a journey which may be hundreds of miles. Eventually it arrives at the bank which ordered it.

(13) At the bank the bag is opened, the cents are dumped out, and quantities of pieces are put into a mechanical counting and wrapping machine, which by means of a tube at the lower end permits 50 coins to be wrapped in a paper roll. Now, and only now, is our typical cent ready to enter circulation, which it does by being paid out by a teller at the bank, or given to a commercial client for use in cash register change.

As you can see, by this time the typical Lincoln cent has had quite an experience. The coin is still Uncirculated; that is, the coin has not yet entered circulation. However, it can have many scuff marks, scrapes, nicks, and other problems and if it has been especially roughly handled it may only be MS-60.

The larger the coin is, the more susceptible it is to damage during the minting and subsequent handling process. In their era, large and heavy coins, such as Morgan silver dollars, sustained much more mint-caused damage than did little coins such as contemporary Indian cents. Dramatic evidence of this is provided by the Treasury release in 1962 of Morgan silver dollar Uncirculated pieces which had never seen the channels of commerce and which had been stored in Treasury vaults since the time of minting. It is probably the case that of certain issues, such as Carson City pieces, of a given 1,000 coins in a mint-sealed bag, only a few dozen would qualify today for the MS-65 grade, and most are MS-60 to MS-63.

Historical Minting Procedures

In colonial America, and at various state-operated mints of the 1780s, coinage was typically executed by human labor. In *The Early Coins of America*, Sylvester S. Crosby quoted a letter from Charles I. Bushnell, who described the procedure used to strike coins at Machin's Mills, a private mint located at Newburgh, New York in the late 1780s:

> The coins were struck by means of a large bar loaded at each end with a 500-pound ball, with ropes attached. Two men were required on each side, making four in all, to strike the pieces, besides the man to set the planchets. The metal of which the coins were struck was composed of old brass cannon and mortars, the zinc from the copper being extracted by smelting in a furnace. About 60 of the coins were struck a minute.

The same reference quotes another letter, this one describing the minting of New Jersey copper coins circa 1786:

> (My mother recalls that when she was a child) she used to go into the house on the adjoining premises to her father's residence in this place to see them make coppers. The business was carried on in a room behind the kitchen. The *modus operand!* was as follows: In the middle of the room was a wooden box or a pit sunk in the floor several feet deep, in the middle of which pit was placed an iron die, the top of

which was about level with the floor of the room. A workman sat on the floor, with his legs inside the pit. He placed the smooth coppers on the die, and when stamped [by the upper die coming downward], brushed them off the die into the pit. The impression on the copper was made by a screw-press which was worked by two men, one at each end of an iron bar or horizontal lever, attached to the screw at the center of its length, which was about nine or 10 feet long. . . The copper when coined was put into kegs and sent off.

When the Philadelphia Mint installed coin presses in 1792, they were powered by human muscle, and the process of rolling metal into strips from which planchets could be cut was achieved by horsepower in the literal sense of the term. In 1793 the Philadelphia Mint produced its first coins for general circulation. In *Penny Whimsy*, Dr. William H. Sheldon wrote of conditions during its early operation:

There is no precise record of just what went on at the Mint during its first year. However, the general conditions under which work was carried on, and some of the difficulties peculiar to the undertaking are known. All employees worked 11 hours a day, 66 hours a week, beginning at six in the morning during the summer and at seven during the winter. Average pay for the coin press operators was $1.29 per day. All power was furnished by horses and human muscle. The rolling machinery (for the manufacture of strips from which planchets were cut) fell short of expectations. For a decade or more there was a chronic and often acute shortage of copper as well as a great variability in the assay and consequently in the color and hardness of that metal. We have only begun the list of hardships and difficulties. The struggle to manufacture copper planchets was apparently heroic.

James Davy, who styled himself as an "efficiency expert," visited the Mint in December 1794 and subsequently sent his observations to the Secretary of State. So far as is known, these are the only firsthand recollections surviving from this particular year:

I shall offer my opinions on the Mint of the United States of America. I find the supply of copper has not been regular, that the power now applied is not adequate, nor are many parts of the machinery adapted for performing the work to the best advantage. Other observations might have been made and improvements suggested if I had seen the whole of the machinery at work, or had the opportunity of a more minute inspection of the Mint. There is no doubt but that the coinage may be much improved, by rendering the cents brighter, and clearer from rough black streaks which much disfigure many of them, the expenses considerably diminished and a greater quantity of coins produced; besides laying a foundation for other important advantages to this country, by adopting the plan herein offered. (Here followed Davy's suggestions.)

During the early years of the Philadelphia Mint, copper supplies were erratic. Sources included reclaimed hoops from wooden barrels, melted-down cannon from the Revolutionary War, copper sheathing from roofs and ship bottoms, and metal taken from other coins and tokens (in one well-known procedure the copper tokens of Talbot, Allum & Lee, New York City merchants, were redeemed by the Mint, and planchets for half cents were cut from the centers of them!).

Copper from such diverse and uncertain sources was apt to vary widely in appearance and texture. As a result, freshly minted cents of the 1790s were often streaked, blackened, or had porous surfaces.

Due to an officers' bonding requirement which was not fulfilled at the outset, the Mint did not strike silver coins until 1794 and gold coins until 1795. The sources for these metals, too, were uncertain, and consisted of foreign coins, raw bullion, jewelry, household items, tableware, and the like. However, the refining process for gold and silver turned out a more consistent product, although not without occasional streaks, fissures, porosity, or traces of black carbon.

For the first several decades of the Mint's operation, silver and gold coins had intrinsic values approximately equal to their face value. Thus, if an overweight coin was produced, it would be quickly extracted from circulation, melted, and converted to bullion which could be sold at a profit. To prevent this, women were employed at the mint to carefully weigh each blank planchet on a pair of balance scales (later, Seyss automatic weighing machines were introduced, but this was not until after the Civil War). If a planchet was found to be underweight, it was rejected and went to the melting pot. More often, a planchet was found to be slightly overweight. In such an instance, a metal file was drawn across the surface, thus removing excess metal and leaving a series of parallel grooves, known by numismatists today as *adjustment marks*. If a planchet had to be filed more than once, the grooves often crossed each other and were at different angles. It is apparent from the examination of surviving coins, particularly those of the 1790s, that the Mint's practice was to make planchets slightly overweight, so they could be adjusted by filing. This was more expedient than trying to make them the precise weight to begin with, for some planchets would inevitably be underweight, and there is no way that metal could be added to an underweight planchet (although apparently an effort was made to add metal to underweight silver dollar planchets in the year 1795). The practice of adjusting planchets by hand continued well into the latter part of the 19th century.

After a planchet was adjusted to the correct weight, it was then a candidate to be put through the edge-lettering machine (a device used for half cents and cents of the early 1790s, for silver half dollars from 1794 through 1836, and for silver dollars from 1794 through 1803). Pieces not requiring lettered edges (such as later cents, half dimes, dimes, quarter dollars, and all gold denominations) were then run through an upsetting machine, to raise the rim, although it is not certain in what year the upsetting machine was first introduced.

After edge lettering or upsetting, the blank planchet or disk was ready for striking. The procedure was strictly a hand-operation in the early days, with each planchet being carefully fed into the press, stamped, and then ejected. The quality of striking varied considerably and depended in part upon the speed in which the press was operated. An even more important consideration was the die spacing. Adjustments were made so that the dies would come close enough together to permit the transfer of the image from each die to the planchet, but not so close that the metal would have nowhere to go except to flow toward the edges. If this happened, then the diameter of the coin would be increased to an unsatisfactory size (in instances in which coins were struck without a collar) or, for later-era pieces made with a reeded restraining collar, such as silver coins without edge lettering and gold coins, the collar and dies would be subjected to early wear and breakage.

A happy medium was achieved, whereby the die spacing was set so that the metal would fill or nearly fill the deepest recesses of the die and there would be no extra metal left to cause collar or die breakage. The result was that coins struck during this era typically were lightly defined in certain areas.

In late 1836, steam-operated presses were installed at the Philadelphia Mint, replacing the earlier hand-operated presses (some of which later saw service at branch mints). With the advent of the steam press, coinage became more uniform. Pressure was constant, as it was applied by a quickly rotating flywheel which moved the top die up and down through a proscribed path of travel. From the standpoint of pressure applied, from this time onward there was no such thing as a "light" or "heavy" strike. Differences in striking details were provided solely by variations in die spacing (or planchet thickness), a concept nearly universally overlooked by numismatic scholars and writers.

In 1838, branch mints were established at Charlotte (North Carolina), Dahlonega (Georgia), and New Orleans, with these branch institutions receiving some obsolete equipment from the Philadelphia Mint, in addition to new equipment. Coinage accomplished at Dahlonega and Charlotte from 1838 until both mints closed in 1861 was crude compared with that of Philadelphia, and today Charlotte and Dahlonega coins often show lack of detail, poor planchets, and other irregularities; characteristics which impart a certain charm to the issues.

Later, branch mints were opened in San Francisco (1854), Carson City (1870), and Denver (1906). Beginning in the 1960s, the United States Bullion Depository at West Point, New York was employed from time to time to produce coins, although no mintmark was used until the 1984-W $10 Olympic commemoratives.

From the earliest times to the present day, the primary thrust of the various mint efforts has been to produce coins for circulation, not to grace the cabinets of numismatists. Such pieces, produced for business purposes, are known today as *business strikes* (as opposed to Proof or specimen issues).

Chapter 8

Specimen and Proof Coins

Beginning in the early days of the Philadelphia Mint, it was customary to strike on special occasions coins which were known as specimen or Proof examples. In a formal sense, Proof coins, characterized by pieces with mirror-like obverse and reverse surfaces, struck from specially prepared planchets and using highly polished dies, were not made until 1817, when special apparatus was installed for that purpose. However, certain earlier coins with prooflike surfaces, such as 1796 quarter dollars, are sometimes catalogued as Proofs. Even though they may not have been made on special Proof presses, such coins were obviously made from specially prepared dies and struck with great care.

Proof coins were produced especially for presentation to government officials, dignitaries, and others of importance, as well as for sale or trade to collectors. A well-known numismatic story relates that Joseph J. Mickley, an early numismatist, visited the Philadelphia Mint in 1827 and received for face value four Proof quarter dollars of that date. Year after year, Proofs were made in limited quantities. During the 1830s, 1840s, and early 1850s it is probably the case that no more than three or four dozen examples were made of each of the various half cent, cent, and other denominations through the silver dollar, and fewer still were made of gold coins. There are a few scattered exceptions, such as the 1836 Gobrecht silver dollar, of which at least 1,600 Proofs were struck, most of which were subsequently placed into circulation at face value.

In 1858, Proofs were first sold to the public. Distribution from that time forward was, with some exceptions, done by selling minor coins (those made of copper or nickel alloy) in sets, silver coins in sets, and gold coins individually. Thus, in the year 1888, 30 years after sets were first publicly sold, minor Proof sets consisting of the Indian cent, nickel three-cent piece, and Liberty Head nickel were made to the extent of 4,582 pieces of each. Silver Proof sets comprising the dime, quarter dollar, half dollar, and silver dollar, were made in the number of 832. Gold Proof coins could be ordered separately and were produced in the following quantities: gold dollars 1,079, quarter eagles 97, $3 pieces 291, half eagles 95, eagles 75, and double eagles 105.

While the Mint produced specified quantities of Proof coins each year, it was often the case that quantities were left unsold by year's end and were melted. So, many Proof coins are rarer than mintage figures indicate.

The Saint-Gaudens gold coinage of 1907 and the Pratt $2.50 and $5 coins of 1908 saw the introduction of new Proof finishes. From then through the next several years Matte Proof, Sandblast Proof, and Roman Finish Proofs were made at the Philadelphia Mint. These new Proofs lacked the mirror-like surface of their earlier counterparts and were derived from processes popularized at the Paris Mint. The new finishes were not popular with collectors, and because of declining sales Proof coinage was suspended after a small production of cents and nickels in 1916.

In 1936, Proofs were again made. As was true of earlier years, Proof coins could be ordered in sets or on an individual basis. From then until 1942, Proofs were made of the denominations from the cent through the half dollar. Production was suspended during World War II, to resume in 1950, after which time Proofs were available only in sets.

Although Proof coins were supposed to have been struck from mirror-like dies, using carefully prepared planchets, and produced to create virtually perfect coins, in practice this was often not the case. In the early days, when the dies were cleaned at intervals by wiping them with an oily rag, residue was often deposited on the die surfaces. As strange as it may seem, a thread or a human hair, left on the surface of a die, can result in its image sharply imprinted into the surface of the coin, causing what today are known as *lint marks*. These are particularly prevalent on Proof coins of the mid 19th century. Sometimes the dies would be improperly spaced, so that on Liberty Seated silver coins, for example, the stars would be lightly struck at the centers, or the features of Miss Liberty would be lightly defined. In other instances, the dies were not given a high polish, and it is possible that specially prepared planchets were not used. As a result, 1878 Shield nickels, for example, an issue of which just Proofs were made (according to Mint records), exist today with frosty surfaces characteristic of Uncirculated business strikes. These are technically Proofs, but if they had been of a date in which business strikes were also made, numismatists would call them Uncirculated.

When Proof sets were made in 1936, following a lapse in Proof coinage since 1916, the first cents and nickels made had frosty rather than mirror-like surfaces, a sort of satin finish. Complaints ensued, and soon the mint corrected the situation.

The foregoing paragraphs reveal that not all Proofs were created equal, nor were all Proofs carefully struck, nor were all made without defects. In addition, the Mint often handled Proofs carelessly, especially during the 19th century. One collector registered a strong complaint when he visited the Philadelphia Mint to buy some Proof gold coins and found that the available specimens were kept loosely jumbled together in a box, so that most showed nicks and scratches!

To the credit of mint employees in modern times, most Proofs made since 1950 are of high quality, and most made since 1968 are of very high quality. There are exceptions, but they are occasional.

Happily, many outstanding Uncirculated and Proof coins have survived the rigors of the minting procedure and the vagaries of the sands of time and have come down to us in outstanding preservation. Survival has not necessarily meant safety, for as the chapters on cleaning and retoning coins in the present text indicate, many fine pieces have been damaged by numismatists, the very people who are supposed to protect them.

The preceding discussion of minting procedures is necessarily an outline. Processes varied over periods of time, as did the care paid to producing coins, the quality of equipment used, and so on. Virtually each decade of coinage, from each different mint, has characteristics which differ from similar pieces produced a decade earlier or later. Among very early coins, the characteristics of die preparation, planchet quality, striking sharpness, and the like vary from coin to coin, even within the same denomination in the same year. One could study the copper cents of 1794, for example, and of the several dozen varieties known, observe differing sharpness, surface coloration, planchet quality, evidence of die wear, and other characteristics.

Chapter 9

Handling, Storing and Displaying Coins

As the owner of a coin, you have an obligation to posterity to be a careful custodian of it. The availability of high-quality coins to future generations is dependent upon how they are handled by numismatists and others today. As related earlier, many beautiful coins of superb quality have been reduced in grade several steps by careless handling by those to whose care they were entrusted.

This chapter gives pointers on how to handle coins carefully and properly, how to package and ship them, how to store them safely, and how to mount them for display.

Handling Coins

It is proper numismatic etiquette to handle another person's coins carefully, whether they are coins of a fellow collector, a dealer who has shown them to you for purchase, a museum, or any other entity. It is also good procedure to handle your own coins carefully, for a careless move can result in damage and a consequent loss of value.

Under all circumstances, a coin should be held carefully by the edge, over a soft surface. Hold the coin close to a cloth, soft pad, or some other soft surface, so if it does fall by accident, no harm will be done. For ease in viewing, a soft pad on a table is ideal. If you are standing and viewing a coin at the same time, the chances are increased that you may drop the coin, and if you do, the coin has a greater chance of being damaged.

Your fingers are acidic, and if you touch a coin other than by its edge, an unsightly fingerprint will result. If you are skeptical, take a modern Lincoln cent and impress your thumb on its surface. Leave it out in the open, then look at it a few weeks later, and you will see every characteristic of your thumbprint in brown. Obviously, if your hands are dirty, clean them before handling coins, even though you plan to handle them by the edges. Even freshly washed hands contain a degree of acid, so adhere to the rule of handling by the edges only.

If you have occasion to touch the obverse or reverse of a coin, such as when pressing it into a holder or album, or testing it for authenticity (refer to our chapter on this subject), then protect your coin by wearing a thin cloth glove, or use a clean rubber glove, or put a piece of dry soft cloth between your fingertip and the coin.

Do not breathe directly on the surface of a coin. When studying a coin under magnification, hold it so that your breath does not fall on the coin, for breath contains minute moisture particles which eventually will cause microscopic spotting. Similarly, do not hold a coin near your mouth when you are talking, for moisture drops will fall on the coin's surface. It is probably the case that the microscopic black oxidation spots often seen today on Proof nickel five-cent pieces of the Shield and Liberty Head types, for example, were caused by such moisture falling on the coins years ago.

For the purposes of studying a coin's surface characteristics and determining its grade, the author has found that a 100-watt *incandescent* bulb, housed in a reflector and positioned two to three feet away from the coin, is ideal. A Tensor-type lamp can also be used. As the wattage of a Tensor lamp is less, the lamp can be moved closer. Under no circumstances should a lamp ever be placed sufficiently close to a coin that the temperature of the coin's surface will increase, otherwise spotting or toning may result.

It is important to have an *incandescent* lamp, as this furnishes a pinpoint source of light. A fluorescent lamp gives a general, nonspecific source of light, and will mask hairlines, evidence of friction, and other defects, making a coin appear to be nicer than it really is, a situation which is particularly true of higher-grade Uncirculated and Proof pieces. Also, a fluorescent lamp, or light, emits fewer colors of the spectrum and therefore does not give you "true" light. If you are offered a coin and no incandescent light is available, insist upon going to a location where an incandescent bulb can be employed.

A hand-held magnifying glass is ideal for examining coins in detail. For years the writer (Q. David Bowers) has used a combination 4X and 8X magnifier with a lens slightly larger than an inch in diameter. A lens of this size permits a sufficient area to be examined in detail, perhaps the entire area of a small coin such as a silver three-cent piece or gold dollar. At the same time, the magnification is sufficient so that hairlines, rubbing, and other attributes are clearly defined. A large library-type reading glass is not strong enough. A tiny loupe-type glass, or any glass which gives extreme magnification, will permit detailed study of a certain feature, such as a mintmark. It will not give a large enough field to determine the general grade. (It is useful to have a stronger glass for studying die characteristics, but this is a subject apart from grading.) If you use a glass with a metal frame, be sure that the metal frame does not come in contact with the coin, or damage can result.

There are three "sides" to a coin—the obverse, the reverse, and the edge. When examining a coin, it is a good idea to check the edge as well. It is sometimes the case that early pieces have marks on the edge which indicate they were once used as jewelry and had a mounting loop. In other instances, forgeries have been made by drilling inward from the edge and by an embossing tool raising a mintmark on a Buffalo nickel, so that a Philadelphia issue magically becomes a "1924-S." Alterations of this type attracted widespread notice beginning in 1986.

Storage

Coin storage is an important consideration, and one which can affect the grade of a coin. If a coin is carefully stored, the grade and value will remain constant. For a carelessly stored coin this may not be the case.

For everyday storage (as opposed to display) many options are available. Years ago, coins were often stored in what was called "tarnish-proof" tissue, and the Philadelphia Mint itself used this for Proof coins during the 1909-1916 era, but it subsequently developed that the sulfur content in such tissue imparted a toning to each piece, an attractive toning, but toning nonetheless. Beginning in 1936, the Philadelphia Mint shipped its Proof coins in cellophane envelopes. It developed that these, too, had problems, and sometimes beads of moisture on the coins were trapped in the cellophane envelopes and later developed into oxidation spots. Also, the glued seams of the cellophane envelopes sometimes caused streaking or spotting. The standard old-time way of storing coins was to house them in paper envelopes measuring two inches square, with a flap at the top. Left alone in these envelopes, copper coins typically retained their brilliance for many years, even decades; nickel coins tended to tone to a gray color, sometimes with hints of brown; silver coins would lightly tone over a period of years, often brown or gold, sometimes lightly mottled; and gold coins would not tone at all. It was popular among certain advanced collectors and connoisseurs to put a small cotton lined envelope within the paper envelope, to protect the surface of the coin. These cotton envelopes seemed to have a neutral effect, and not much change was observed for coins kept in such envelopes over a period of time. So much for storage methods of "the good old days."

Today the numismatist has many other options. Paper envelopes still exist and are favored by many, for they permit a writing surface to record details such as grades, price, cost, source, etc. For pieces in grades less than Uncirculated or Proof state, with surfaces which no longer have mint brilliance, such envelopes are very handy.

Cardboard holders measuring approximately two inches square (although they are made in other sizes as well), with clear cellophane or other plastic covering a circular hole at the center, are made in several varieties. Some are self-sealing and have glue around the edges, whereas others must be sealed with staples. Such holders are quite popular and serve to protect a coin against handling, although there are scattered reports of the glue-seal type discoloring coins. There is a distinct danger in using the staple type, in that when a coin is removed from a stapled holder, great care must be taken to prevent the coin from coming into contact with the staple ends. Using a staple remover may seem obvious, but most people find that a staple remover is not at hand when it is time to open a holder. One well-known numismatist had the unfortunate experience of brushing a superb Proof 1863 quarter eagle against a staple end, thus putting a scratch on it which diminished its value by many thousands of dollars. If you use stapled holders be very careful!

Flexible translucent polyethylene envelopes, the type sold by Whitman and certain others, are very satisfactory for the protection of coins, and are handy for keeping inside another container, such as a paper envelope. Polyethylene is inert, and coins stored this way will maintain their surface characteristics for an indefinite period.

The disadvantage is that the translucent envelope does not permit inspection of the coin except by removal, not a consideration if you are a collector, but if you are a dealer it can be annoying to constantly remove and insert coins. Polyethylene envelopes are highly recommended.

Snap-together coin holders, slightly larger than the diameter of the coin, and consisting of an obverse and reverse "lens" which can snap together over the coin, the popular "Koin-Tain" brand being an example, are an effective way of protecting coins so they can be displayed at the same time. However, it is then necessary to place the Koin-Tain or similar device within a paper envelope or some other container so it can be stored and classified properly, otherwise the holders would soon arrange themselves into a loose jumble.

Mylar "flips" became popular in the late 1980s. These consist of a two-part device with a pocket on each side; one pocket for storing the coin, and another pocket for the insertion of a slip of paper or cardboard upon which can be written information concerning price, rarity, source, grade, etc. These mylar "flips" are excellent in that they permit a clear view of the coin, but disadvantages are that they often crack along the edge (particularly when heavy coins such as double eagles or silver dollars are stored in them), and the two pockets do not come together in a parallel manner, but instead tend to maintain a V-shape, which makes storage of just a few "flips" a clumsy situation. If many flips are compressed together in a coin storage box, the problem is minimized. "Flips" were made as a substitute for vinyl holders (see following paragraph), which were in wide use in the 1970s and early 1980s, but which subsequently proved to have a major problem. "Flips" are very popular with the dealer community, but less so with the collecting fraternity.

Soft vinyl envelopes are clear and permit examination of a coin. Their flexible surfaces are gentle on the coins contained therein. Made with two pockets, one for a coin and the other for a card, such envelopes were very popular during the 1970s and early 1980s, until it was discovered that over a period of time a gooey substance, polyvinyl chloride (PVC), coated the coin. With copper and nickel coins, this effected a change in the surface characteristics and resulted in changing brilliant coins to a greenish brown. For silver coins, the coating had a less harmful effect, and for gold coins there was not much of a problem. It developed that PVC could be removed by the judicious application of acetone (which, as noted, should only be used while observing stringent precautions), but for certain coins, particularly copper-nickel issues, permanent damage had been done. Today, PVC holders are still sometimes used for the showing of auction lots, where many people want to examine a given coin, and the coin must be protected from harm, but it is common practice for the auction companies to warn that such envelopes should not be used for long-term storage. Similarly, the American Numismatic Association Certification Service and the American Numismatic Association Grading Service were using PVC-content envelopes in the 1970s and 1980s but warned that they were not suitable for anything other than short-term purposes. For storing in a collection, PVC-content envelopes are not recommended under any circumstances, and coins bought at auction or elsewhere in these envelopes should be removed from PVC-content envelopes as soon as possible.

Individual coins can be protected by coating them with clear fingernail polish on both sides and the edge. This method will preserve the brilliance, even of copper coins, for many decades. The clear fingernail polish can be removed easily with nail polish remover. A protective coating is given to the coin which will stand as a guard against the friction of album slides (about which more will be written later) or careless handling. A disadvantage is that certain minute grading details, such as hairlines, are apt to be masked by the coating. If you apply clear fingernail polish after buying the coin, there is no problem. However, you may wish to use caution if buying a previously coated coin.

Many collectors and investors have found that aluminum foil, if carefully wrapped around the coin, will protect it against atmospheric considerations and will maintain the brilliance of the coin for a long time. While this might be fine for Uncirculated coins with lustre, we hesitate recommending its use for Proofs, for the metallic contact of the foil with the delicate Proof surface may cause minor hairlines. Foil is mentioned here as a method popular with some, but it is not recommended.

Rigid plastic holders of various types are available on the market. Several dealers, grading services, and others have hermetically sealed coins in rigid holders, with the thought that a coin thus sealed maintains a constant grade and, thus, can be bought or sold sometime in the future without having to grade it again. This theory is fine, but in practice there are occasional flaws. First, sometimes hermetically sealed holders come apart at the edge, permitting other coins to be substituted. Another problem with hermetically sealed holders is that the edge cannot be examined, and any edge defects are thus concealed. If the defects are discovered later, it might be too late to make an adjustment if the return period has expired, or the seller has gone out of business. Further, hermetically sealed holders are clumsy, and while they are fine for protection, they tend to slip and slide against each other and are not particularly desirable for display. Thus, in all instances we recommend letting a coin stand on its own, and applying your own grade before buying it. A crummy coin in a fancy holder is still a crummy coin! As of the late 1980s, their main appeal has been the investor (rather than collector) market.

Rigid plastic holders secured with metal or plastic screws at the corners are another way to store coins. These are available in small sizes, suitable for individual coin use, and are an excellent protection against atmospheric considerations. The screws permit removal of the coin at any time so that the edge can be examined or so that a closer view of the piece can be obtained.

In any and every instance, before putting a coin into a container, be sure that it is absolutely dry. Any dampness, traces of grease or oil, or other substance on a coin will, if put with a coin in a holder, cause problems, including spotting and oxidation.

In all instances, coins should be kept in a favorable atmosphere. Industrial fumes, particularly those containing sulfur, will tone a coin over a period of time. Damp air will have an unfavorable effect, particularly on copper and nickel coins, and will cause oxidation and spotting. Damp air containing microscopic traces of salt, such as is found at the seashore, will also damage a coin's surface. In large cities, smog, which contains acids, will discolor a coin. The effects of dampness, microscopic salt particles, smog, and industrial fumes can be minimized by putting a coin in an airtight holder, but even so the holder itself should be stored in a dry, clean atmosphere.

Bank vaults, particularly those underground, can be damp. If your bank vault is damp, the best alternative is to move to another vault which is dry. If this is not possible, the dampness can be removed to an extent by putting a packet of silica gel in the box (silica gel is available at photographic supply stores). The silica gel absorbs moisture and must be changed from time to time.

If you live in a pleasant, dry atmosphere, and if you keep your coins in plastic, polyethylene, mylar, NGC or PCGS "slabs," or Koin-Tain holders, there is not much to worry about. However, if you live in a smog-laden downtown area, by the seashore, or in a damp locality, it is wise to take certain precautions just noted. Your local coin dealer can be helpful in his regard. Ask his advice, for chances are excellent that he can recommend products which have proven their worth in your vicinity.

Coin Display

"If you have it, display it!" If you own choice, rare, and desirable coins, it is natural to want to display them in an attractive way.

Even if you show them to no one else, there is a certain satisfaction in having a holder or album page which shows before you all at once, in neat order, the different dates in a set of Liberty Head nickels, or 20th-century United States coins by design types, or some other specialty. There is not much "fun" in looking at a bunch of loose holders, paper envelopes, or other individually housed pieces.

Years ago, there were many excellent albums on the market which were popular for storage and display. Cardboard albums with acetate (later, inert plastic) sliders were marketed by M.L. Beistle, Wynne, and Wayte Raymond ("National" brand) in the late 1920s and 1930s. Later, related products such as Meghrig holders (close copies of the Raymond "National" holders), the "Popular" albums, the "Library of Coins" albums, Dansco albums and the Whitman "Bookshelf" albums each achieved a measure of popularity. Warning: the previously mentioned albums with acetate or plastic slides can cause damage to coins if not used carefully. Believe it or not, a clear plastic slide, if drawn against the face of a Proof coin (such as a Barber coin or Franklin half dollar), can leave a series of parallel microscopic scratches! If you are in doubt, experiment yourself by using a modern Proof set of low value (on second thought, take our word for it, for we would dislike to see even a modern Proof set damaged). So, when using these albums, press the coin deeply into the hole (wearing a protective cloth or rubber glove, or by putting a piece of tissue or cloth between your finger and the coin) before inserting the slide. When removing the slide, be sure that each coin is pressed down into its opening—this can be done by pressing the coin through the slide. Failure to do this may cause problems.

Beginning a generation ago, collectors became very conscious of the "brilliant" aspect of coins, and toning was regarded as undesirable. Although this question has more than one side, many numismatists, particularly those who had been at the game for more than a few years, believed that toning is desirable. The public was conditioned to believe that "brilliant is best" and "toning is terrible." The previously mentioned albums, made of cardboard with some sulfur content, tended to impart a toning to the coins, beginning from the edge and continuing toward the center. Today, few such albums are available, although the Dansco brand lingers on and is appreciated by those who use it.

In our opinion, the old Raymond, Meghrig, and related albums are excellent for the storage and display of coins. Those concerned with toning have but to coat coins with clear fingernail polish to solve the toning "problem." However, few such albums are available on the market today, so unless you locate some from an unsold stock from years ago, you may be out of luck.

Harco, Eagle, and others have manufactured combination holders which consist of album pages in which individual plastic holders can be mounted. Thus, the coins are housed in individual square-shaped holders, and the square-shaped holders themselves are fitted into larger album pages. The result is an arrangement which serves to satisfactorily protect the coins (although some earlier versions of the Harco holders, now off the market, contain PVC—so don't use these), but for some they lacked an aesthetic appeal. Still, such assembly type albums may be useful during the building stages of a collection. Your best bet is to check out available holders of this type and see which are aesthetically pleasing to you.

For museum-quality display, Capital Plastic (to mention the leading firm in business when the present text was prepared) and other firms have on the market a series of three-part Lucite holders. Typically, such holders consist of a central piece with circular openings for coins, such central piece being either silk-screened or gold-imprinted with information about the coin, such as the date and mintmark variety. This central piece is sandwiched between two clear outer layers and secured with plastic or metal screws.

The advantage of these holders is that they are very beautiful and serve to showcase a fine collection. At the same time, they act as a protective element and keep the coins free from the atmosphere, from handling, and other negative effects.

The disadvantages of these holders is that they are fairly expensive (with many of them selling within the range of $20 to

$40 each), and that during the collection building process, the constant opening and closing of such a holder can be a clumsy affair. Our recommendation is to use another method of storage for individual coins during the building process. When the collection is complete, or nearly complete, then transfer it to a large plastic display holder. The cost of such a holder will probably be little when compared with the value of the coins it contains. The aesthetic benefits will repay the plastic holder's costs many times over.

The state of the art in coin storage products and display holders is constantly changing, and it may be the case that by the time you read this there may be newer and better products available. Also, the author is not familiar with each and every type of container on the market, and it may be that other types of holders which are equally or more satisfactory than those mentioned here may exist. We recommend that you investigate the situation thoroughly, and that you consult with your local dealer for additional ideas.

Shipping Coins

Many coin transactions are conducted by mail. Insured registered mail is a safe way to transport coins from one place to another, perhaps the very safest way. The story has often been told of Harry Winston, who donated the Hope Diamond to the Smithsonian Institution, and who desired to transport it from New York City to Washington. He investigated several methods, including armored vehicle, courier, and mail, and decided to send it by insured registered mail. He did this, and the diamond arrived safely. Dealers and collectors who buy coins at conventions or at auctions often have their purchases shipped to themselves by insured registered mail, to avoid the security risks of personal transit. Alternative methods, particularly for shipping larger quantities, include armored car services and various air express agencies. In any event, before shipping coins by any method, check with the shipper to determine packaging and weight requirements, insurance availability, delivery schedules, and other things you need to know.

When shipping coins it is best not to have the word "coins" or "numismatics" appear anywhere on the outside of the shipping container or package. If you are shipping coins to the Ace Coin Company (a name we made up) at 1234 Main Street, Centerville, Iowa, simply delete the word "Coins" from the title and address it to the Ace Company. It will get there. Mentioning "coins," "gold," "numismatics," "bullion," or some other term referring to the value of the contents is just asking for trouble! Even professional rare coin companies often avoid using the "coin" part of their name on packages sent out.

When preparing a package for shipment, be sure each coin in the package is individually wrapped, preferably in an individual holder. Never ship coins loose, for they will rub against each other and will be damaged. The best method is to put them in individual envelopes or holders, and then put the individual holders within a sturdy cardboard box or a specially constructed mailing envelope (such as the Saf-T-Mailer used by many dealers). Create a "package within a package," so that the recipient, upon opening the package, will find an inner package containing the coins desired. Do not scatter coins or holders loose among packing material.

Enclose an inventory with the coins shipped, and keep a duplicate inventory for your own records. In that way the recipient will know what coins are supposed to be in the package, and can verify that all are actually there. Obviously the package itself should be clearly and properly addressed, with your return address on the outside and inside, and that appropriate postage and registration fees should be affixed. Check with the post office first if you have doubt concerning any aspect of packaging.

If you have coins for sale, do not send them unsolicited, for the intended buyer may be away, or in any event the buyer may not wish to purchase them. Years ago, B. Max Mehl and other dealers who used to do a large volume of buying by mail used to always say "write first." If you want to sell coins, telephone or write the dealer or collector first to be sure that the coins are wanted. Otherwise you are just wasting time and postage.

When you receive a package in the mail, open it carefully by hand (do not employ any mechanical device in this regard). First order of business, compare the contents with the inventory. If there is any problem, notify the sender immediately, and in the meantime keep all the wrappings.

Shipping coins by mail is a procedure tested by time, and it is probably the case that most major collections have been built at least in part by the purchase of coins through the mail. Observe the several sensible precautions noted, and you should have no problems at all.

Chapter 10

Cleaning Coins

Ever since day one, collectors and dealers have experimented with cleaning coins. To the uninitiated, "brilliant" means "better." From the 1950s through the 1970s, when numbers were rarely used in connection with grading coins (except for large cents), the adjective "brilliant" often implied that a coin was among the best of its kind. Thus, an 1880 silver dollar described as Uncirculated would be an average coin in the mind of a buyer or seller, where as one described as "Brilliant Uncirculated" would be an especially nice piece. Similarly, "brilliant" was used in connection with Proof coins. Today, the prevalent philosophy is different, and often a coin with attractive toning will sell for more than a brilliant one.

In numismatic literature many references to cleaning coins can be found. In 1878 a vast treasure of over 100,000 early American silver coins came to light in Economy, Pennsylvania. This treasure or hoard was secreted by the Harmony Society during the Civil War to prevent seizure. When the silver pieces came to light, years later in 1878, they were tarnished from dampness and oxidation. The first thing the residents of Economy did was to scrub each one to make it brilliant. The result was that many desirable pieces had their values lessened to collectors, who considered them impaired.

In *Penny Whimsy*, Dr. William H. Sheldon noted:

> "Many a cent has been ruined by an attempt to improve it. Amateurs, and some who are not so amateur, are forever trying to improve the condition or appearance of an old cent." The writer went on to tell of pieces which have been "transformed into a brassy nightmare by some well intentioned effort to 'clean' it, perhaps with acid or an eraser; or even with a buffing wheel (it has been done!). When this tragedy has happened the coin may be numismatically

worthless unless it can be recolored and again be made, to some extent, to look like old copper...."

Many products for cleaning coins are available on the market, and in some instances the representation is made that the use of such products will enhance a coin's value. At one time a "kit" was offered, consisting of a brass wire brush in combination with a cleaning solution. The statement was made that by using the kit an "ugly" old copper coin could be transformed to a brilliant, and thus desirable piece. Left unstated was the fact that most experienced collectors of copper coins would not have touched the resultant coin with a 10-foot pole!

Although many other examples and quotations could be given concerning the harm done by cleaning coins, human nature being what it is, you may be tempted to try your hand at the cleaning process. If you do, consider the subject carefully. Probably for every one coin "improved" by cleaning, ten or more have had their values lessened.

Cleaning, when necessary, should be done only with nickel, silver, and gold coins in top grades. To clean such pieces in grades less than About Uncirculated will produce an unnatural appearance that is not acceptable to most collectors. The cleaning of copper and bronze coins in any condition should be avoided unless it is necessary to remove an unsightly carbon spot or fingerprint. In all instances, practice cleaning methods with low-value coins, so if you ruin them, they can simply be spent!

To clean a high-grade nickel, silver, or gold coin, use only a clear liquid "dip," not a paste, powder, or polish. Pour some dip, full strength, into a pliable plastic dish. Completely immerse the coin in the liquid. Do not leave the coin in the liquid longer than a few seconds. Immediately rinse the coin thoroughly under running cold water. Pat (do not rub) the coin dry with a soft absorbent cloth; a terry cloth towel is ideal. Holding the coin in your fingers and using a cotton swab may result in uneven cleaning. For copper coins, if you must experiment with them, use a mixture of half "dip" and half cold water.

In lieu of rinsing the coin for a long period of time under running cold water, the "dip" can be neutralized somewhat by immersing the coin, after dipping, in water in which a generous amount of baking soda has been dissolved. Swish the coin around in the water, remove it, and then hold it under running cold water. After drying the coin with a soft absorbent cloth, be sure there is no moisture adhering to the surfaces. It is a good idea to allow the coin to remain exposed to the open atmosphere for an hour or more before encasing it in an airtight holder. Trace amounts of "dip" adhering to a coin's surface will eventually tarnish or corrode the coin.

The "dip" acts on the coin's surface by removing the tarnish and, at the same time, minute parts of the coin's metal. If a silver coin is dipped repeatedly, it will take on a dull, gray appearance. Under magnification, the mirror surface of a Proof coin will be seen to be finely etched, resulting in a cloudy surface which cannot be corrected.

In the cleaning of a coin, never use any substance which requires friction. To be avoided are jeweler's rouge, silver-cleaning paste, baking soda, salt, or any similar substances. These substances clean coins by forcibly removing metal from the surface. The result will be a coin showing many hairlines. The application of a cleaning paste to a Proof coin can reduce its value to a tiny fraction of what would have been otherwise.

It is sometimes desirable on circulated coins, Uncirculated coins, and Proofs as well, to remove a light film of dirt, grease, or PVC residue (the latter from storing coins in plastic holders which over a period of time exude a substance which forms a greenish coating on coins). Residues from tape, spots of glue, and other substances are sometimes found on coin surfaces and need to be removed. A commercial solvent, acetone, a chemical available at drug stores, will usually do the trick. Acetone is highly flammable and gives off fumes which should not be inhaled. Use acetone only in an open area, well ventilated, and away from spark or flame. Do not treat acetone casually. The removal of dirt, grit, and other verdigris, which sometimes accumulates on the surface of a coin, particularly one which has been in circulation for many years, can be done by using an ultrasonic cleaning machine in combination with a solution which does not change the surface coloration. Jewelers commonly use such devices to clean dirty rings, bracelets, and the like. Cleaning with acetone or by ultrasonic methods is different from dipping, for the latter methods simply remove dirt or residue without affecting the toning or coloration of a coin.

In general, dipping and cleaning to change the color of a coin's surface is undesirable; removing dirt and residue is desirable.

An excellent commentary on the subject of cleaning coins was furnished by John J. Ford, Jr. in a column in *Numisma* in the 1950s. The philosophy is unchanged today:

> There are as many "expert" ways to clean coins as there are coin dealers. We suggest you read Dr. Sheldon's comments in his book, and talk to older, experienced collectors. Well toned coins, strictly Uncirculated or Proof and without blemishes, are valued more highly by us than the usually found "cleaned" silver examples. It is almost inevitable that a really old silver coin which has so-called brilliance must have been meticulously cleaned so as to seem so. The aluminum pan with baking soda in solution, often used for cleaning silverware, is good for ordinary dull tarnish and is probably the commonest method, as well as one of the safest...

> For my money, "expert cleaning" leaves the coin looking as if it *had not been touched.* In this light, we suggest coins with an even and attractively colored toning be left alone, as it will for a long time protect them against less desirable tarnish

> Abrasives of any sort are dangerous. Jeweler's rouge is to be avoided; it is simply iron oxide (rust) ground to fine powder, and its action is simply scouring...

> Proofs are no different from other coins, except they show the results of sloppy cleaning more easily. We do not retouch 99% of the material we handle, except for an occasional brushing, or the judicious use of a little mineral oil. To sum it up, it is much better to leave "improving" to the other fellow, as well as the "expert" designation in this field of endeavor.

Having given you ample warning, but with the realization that on occasion cleaning can be desirable, we now discuss cleaning of various coins.

Cleaning Copper and Bronze Coins

The "dipping" or chemical cleaning of copper and bronze coins is to be avoided. The only exceptions, and such exceptions are rare, are coins which have unsightly fingerprints, blotches, or areas of oxidation. Cleaning by dipping, following the procedure outlined earlier, will result in the surface becoming bright yellow or orange, an unnatural hue quite unlike a normal uncleaned coin. As such, a piece then becomes a candidate for judicious retoning (see the following section). Under no circumstances should a *worn* copper or bronze coin be dipped or chemically cleaned, for the result will be a bright and unnatural color. Worn copper coins in their natural state are toned varying shades from black to light brown; this natural toning will be destroyed by dipping.

The removal of dirt, green PVC goo, grease, and other substances adhering to the surface of a coin can be accomplished by use of acetone (using it in a well-ventilated area, away from flame), or in some instances simply by the application of soap and water. A bath in a cleaning solution (but not a solution which will remove toning) in a jeweler's ultrasonic cleaner may likewise be desirable. None of these methods will remove toning or change the basic surface color.

After dirt has been removed from the surface of a copper coin, it can be given a glossy surface by brushing it carefully with a No. 4 jeweler's camel hair brush; a method employed by many collectors of early half cents and large cents, or by gentle rubbing with a soft cloth lightly treated with mineral oil or with a liquid product called "Care."

Cleaning Nickel Coins

What we call "nickel" coins are primarily copper. For example, nickel three-cent pieces minted from 1865 to 1889 and nickel five-cent pieces produced beginning in 1866 are composed of three parts copper and one part nickel. If a nickel coin displays unsightly toning blotches, oxidation areas, or unsightly fingerprints, the surface can sometimes be made brilliant by immersing in a liquid "dip."

Nickel coins are more chemically active than silver or gold, so it becomes even more critical to neutralize the "dip" by immersing the coins in cold running water for a long period of time, and then drying each piece thoroughly. Failure to do this will result in the coin acquiring unsightly brown blotches within a matter of weeks. If a nickel coin is dipped more than two or three times, it will become cloudy and soon will have a "cleaned" appearance. As is true with copper and bronze coins, the typical nickel coin is best left uncleaned.

Grease, PVC goo, and dirt can be removed by the judicious application of acetone (again we mention that this substance must be used carefully, in well-ventilated areas and away from flame), by ultrasonic cleaning, or by soap and water. None of these processes is harmful to the coin, and such treatment is recommended in indicated cases.

Cleaning Silver Coins

Think twice, and then think again, before immersing any silver coin in "dip," for it is often the case that attractive toning on a silver coin will increase its value. Dipping of silver coins is recommended only to remove unsightly or blotchy spotting, fingerprints, or oxidation. In these instances, use silver "dip" following the methods outlined earlier. If a silver coin has very deep surface tarnish, deep gray or even coal black, the removal of this tarnish or toning will usually result in leaving a cloudy, etched surface. Cleaning a heavily toned silver coin usually has unfavorable results.

In instances in which a silver coin has surface dirt, PVC goo, or residue, the judicious application of the dangerous substance, acetone (note the safety precautions mentioned earlier), or the use of a jeweler's ultrasonic bath, or the application of soap and water will have favorable results and is recommended.

Cleaning Gold Coins

Of all metals used in United States coinage—copper, nickel, silver, and gold—gold is the most inert. In general, gold coins retain their brilliance for many decades, even centuries. As United States gold coins consist of nine parts gold and one part copper, the copper alloy will cause a light toning over a period of time, so that early pieces often obtain a warm rosy or golden appearance. This is desirable and should not be changed.

The use of a "dip" on gold coins will make the surface brilliant, sometimes brassy in appearance, which for very early pieces is not desirable. Dipping can sometimes remove copper-colored spots or staining occasionally seen on coins, the result of an imperfect alloy mixture, although such removal is by no means guaranteed.

The removal of surface film, dirt, and grease from gold coins can be accomplished with acetone (note the safety precautions mentioned earlier), a jeweler's ultrasonic bath, or soap and water. Ammonia, carefully applied to a coin's surface, can remove a film which sometimes is seen on higher-grade pieces, including Proofs. In all instances, avoid rubbing or the use of friction as this will generate undesirable hairlines.

Chapter 11

Retoning Coins

The retoning of coins is a large subject and covers a multitude of considerations. If a coin has been overly dipped, or cleaned with an abrasive, or rendered an unsightly color, then careful retoning might be able to impart most if not all of its original appeal. There is another aspect of retoning which is not so favorable, and that concerns the application of color or toning to a coin's surface to disguise its true grade, to conceal wear, or to otherwise cause misrepresentation.

As a starting point, consider a coin which has been dipped, scrubbed, or otherwise given a bright or brilliant surface instead of the attractively toned finish it should have. There is no guarantee that the application of any of the following methods will actually improve a coin. In some instances, the result might simply be a blotchy mess! The comments given are for information only. If you must experiment, consult an experienced collector or dealer before attempting to retone a coin of high value.

Retoning Copper and Bronze Coins

When dipped, copper and bronze coins acquire an unnatural brassy color. Nothing is more abhorrent to the connoisseur than to see what would otherwise be an attractive Very Fine or Extremely Fine early large cent which has been scrubbed or dipped to a bright brassy or orange hue. To undo such damage, Dr. William H. Sheldon, in *Penny Whimsy*, presented several ideas, which are reiterated here. His commentary was preceded by a caveat:

> In spite of what you may be told there is no known way of perfectly simulating the natural color that results from slow aging of copper. The student of cents can invariably recognize a "tampered" coin and he almost invariably will

avoid buying it if he can get another, unspoiled, one of the variety. In the course of many years, however, a recolored coin sometimes tends to return gradually to a natural coppery appearance, and as it does so its numismatic value returns also. Therefore if you have a rare cent that has been cleaned, perhaps the best thing to do will be first to experiment with some cheap or modern copper coins then try to recolor it. If it is of excessive rarity, send it to a professional cent recolorer, of whom there are four or five about the country.

There are a dozen or more everyday or "home" methods of trying to recolor cents, none will be found very satisfactory. However, for what they are worth, here a few of them:

(1) Make a mixture of one part fuller's earth with about 10 parts ordinary sifted earth, add water, knead into a sort of doughy biscuit. Insert the cent into this biscuit and bake it slowly in an oven for several hours or leave it on the back of the stove for a week. After the biscuit has slowly cooled, break it open, take out the cent, brush it lightly, and leave it in sunlight for several days. It will then sometimes take on a rather attractive, somewhat natural coppery color, usually with a faint and undesirable iridescence.

(2) Place aqueous ammonia in a small open vessel on a plate. Over the open vessel, but on the plate, invert an ordinary drinking glass or larger utensil. Within the inverted utensil you will then have an atmosphere of concentrated ammonia vapor. The cent should be held on some sort of a makeshift rack within this vapor, for possibly an hour. The result will be an unattractive brownish color, which if allowed to deepen (by leaving the cent longer in the vapor) will take on a decidedly unattractive reddish tint. This method has been widely used for "improving" cents, and has spoiled more than its share of good specimens.

(3) Essentially the same method as the last can be employed, substituting powdered sulfur for the ammonia, but in this instance a degree of heat will be needed. The sulfur can be put into a perforated cardboard box, or ordinary salt shaker,

and the whole apparatus then left on or near the radiator for a day or so. If the process is carried a little too far, the result will be a sort of dirty black color, but if watched closely, a kind of dark iridescence may be achieved which will take on a glossy polish when lightly brushed.

(4) A variation of the sulfur treatment is simply to rub the clean, dry coin lightly with a cotton pledget which has been dipped and powdered in sulfur. This method has the advantage of extreme simplicity, and also one can watch the coin closely as to observe exactly what is going on.

(5) A further variation of the sulfur method, particularly useful for touching up fresh scratches and similar minor injuries to color, is this: Place the coin between two pieces of an old inner tube (if it is made of rubber, not plastic), under a weight of some sort, and leave in a warm place or over a radiator for a day or so. The rubber contains a small amount of sulfur. This is the slowest of the sulfur methods, and it is likely to yield the most even result. But remember that the effect of sulfur, in the final analysis, is simply that of blackening copper.

(6) A method employed by several collectors (and dealers) of the older generation was that of wrapping the coin in a small piece of flannel and, after attaching it to a sort of string belt, wearing it around the waist next to the skin for a matter of a few weeks. Dr. French used to say this method was more efficacious in winter than in summer — winter underclothing holds the sweat better. The underclothing should of course under no circumstances be removed or changed until a satisfactory color has been achieved (!).

(7) Another method is to simply wrap the coin lightly in porous tissue paper and bury it in a flower pot filled with sifted earth. Water the earth from time to time. This experiment will generally require several weeks for good results, but will yield perhaps the nearest obtainable approach to natural aging of copper. A somewhat similar procedure is that of simply exposing the coin to the sun and the weather for a few weeks.

One old-time dealer retoned cleaned large cents by leaving them out of doors for several weeks. At one time he had a particularly desirable 1793 large cent, a rare and valuable coin, but, unfortunately some previous owner had cleaned it to an unnatural orange color. Seeking to restore it to an attractive hue, he put it just outside a window, and forgot about it. In the meantime, unknown to him, a team of workmen was repainting the exteriors of the various rented town houses in the area in which he lived. You guessed it. One day he came home to find his house freshly painted, with no sign of the 1793 cent!

Uncirculated or Proof copper coins which have been dipped or artificially brightened can be retoned to a glossy brown or gray-brown surface using certain methods outlined by Dr. Sheldon. If it is desirable to retain surface brilliance, in combination with what seems to be light "natural" toning, this can be done by exposing the coin to the atmosphere and keeping an eye on it until the right degree of toning is achieved. Make some sort of a suspension device, possibly from a paper clip or of plastic, so that both sides of the coin can be exposed at the same time; otherwise one side will tone and the other will remain bright. Before embarking on the toning process, clean the coin with soap and water or with acetone (observing the important safety precautions described earlier) to remove any surface grease or dirt. Grease adhering to the surface will prevent retoning and will cause blotchiness, for areas covered by the grease will remain bright, whereas areas not overlaid with grease will tone.

The application of slow heat will accelerate the process. One dealer achieved success by balancing cleaned coins on a low-wattage light bulb and then checking the toning every minute or so, removing each coin at the proper instant. An old-time collector's method was to put cleaned cents in a cardboard "National" holder of the type sold by Wayte Raymond years ago, and then heat it for a long time at a low or "warming" temperature in an oven. Gradually, each coin toned from the rim toward the center, giving a pleasing appearance. Be careful, however, for certain old holders have acetate slides protecting the coins, and acetate is highly inflammable, indeed virtually explosive. If you elect to go this route, it would be best to remove the old acetate slides and replace them with thin, clear plastic. This method has its dangers, not the least of which can be ruining the coin by inadvertent over-heating.

Holding a coin by the edges, using a pair of tongs, over iodine fumes can impart an iridescent color to the coin's surface. Iodine fumes are poisonous, so we do not recommend trying this.

As Dr. Sheldon has stated clearly, no matter what retoning methods you use, the chances of restoring the coin to its original desirability are not great. However, there is no doubt that a judiciously retoned coin is more desirable than an unsightly bright one. Before retoning a rare early coin, experiment with low-value modern pieces.

Retoning Nickel Coins

Nickel coins which have been dipped or artificially brightened can be retoned by exposing them to the atmosphere for a length of time, much in the manner of copper coins. The retoning process is more sensitive for nickel coins, and often retoned pieces will exhibit streaking or spotting, thus necessitating redipping and then more retoning, which can be a vicious circle.

One experimenter found that heating nickel coins at low temperature in a frying pan, with cooking grease, yielded various shades of brown and light purple. For nickel coins, experimentation is probably the best procedure, for we are not aware of any dependable method outlined in the literature.

Retoning Silver Coins

The retoning and coloring of silver coins has been developed to a high "art" by some. While retoning may be desirable to restore the surface of a dipped or overly cleaned coin, others employ retoning in an effort to disguise surface marks and friction. Often the retoning is employed with other methods for disguising or improving a coin's surface.

On Morgan silver dollars, Barber silver coins, and other issues, the cheek of Miss Liberty often shows friction, while the fields can remain frosty. Thus, the high parts of the coin will appear abraded or slightly worn, while the protected parts will have the characteristics of a much finer specimen. In an effort to upgrade the appearance of the entire coin, several methods have been employed by various sellers.

Years ago, pieces were commonly dipped in cyanide (a poisonous and sometimes fatal substance; a chemical not recommended under any circumstances), thereby etching all the surfaces, high and low, obliterating hairlines and scuff marks. In the 1950s a refinement on this was tried, whereby the already satisfactory fields and certain other areas of a coin were protected by coating the piece with wax, then immersing the coin in cyanide, so the cheek of Miss Liberty and other scuffed parts would be etched, but the remainder of the coin would stay as is. Sometimes other substances, such as the acid aqua regia, were employed.

Coins subjected to such treatment have a matte or grainy surface where the etching took place, a characteristic which to the expert appears different from the coruscating frost and lustre seen on a piece which has never been tampered with.

Others have "improved" coins by taking a tiny hand-held motorized tool, the type used by jewelers for polishing or by home hobbyist for model building, and carefully wire brushing the high points of a coin, to remove nicks and scratches. The fields are left alone. Again, mint lustre and coruscating frost is absent. However, sometimes lustre and frost can also be added artificially. This is done by taking a wire brush and touching it to the surface in a series of arc-like or curved motions. Under high magnification, the wire brush marks will be evident as furrows in the coin. This process, sometimes employed on the entire surface of a coin, is known as "whizzing," a fraudulent alteration which reached epidemic proportions in the hobby in the early 1970s, when Virgil Hancock and certain others took the matter into their hands, and conducted an investigation, which had the successful result that several "whizzing factories" were put out of business.

The American Numismatic Association Grading Service has reported the existence of a method known as "thumbing," which is employed on Morgan dollars and other coins to erase or hide traces of friction and marks on the high part of a coin's surface.

By this method, gentle pressure, in a rotating movement, is applied to the cheek of a Morgan silver dollar or other coin, using the thumb. Sometimes a fine scouring powder or chemical is also employed. Done carefully, the result is the removal of obvious friction, replacing it with a dull finish which may be more acceptable to the uninitiated buyer.

Each of the foregoing "improvement" processes is discussed here so you can be aware of what you may encounter while buying coins. The preparers of this book do not recommend engaging in whizzing, surface polishing, or any other activity which would distort the true grade of a coin.

Retoning of silver coins can be accomplished in many different ways. Subjecting coins to heat in a frying pan or on a hot plate over a period of time will result in accelerating the atmospheric effects on a coin, changing the surface to brown, iridescent blue, or some other color. Coins that are "fried" sometimes have a gray or gray-blue appearance.

Beginning in the 1980s, a new method of retoning silver coins became popular. Clorox, a commercial bleach, was used to "paint" a coin's surface, thus dulling any bright nicks or marks. If completely coated with Clorox, a coin takes on a light gray tone, which can be quite deceptive in some instances. This is evidenced by an article which appeared in the April 22, 1987 issue of *Coin World*, outlining a suit between two dealers. According to an affidavit, it was stated that one dealer "had treated coins with chemicals so they looked more valuable than they were, has bleached ('Cloroxed') coins to hide imperfections, then charged for them as if the imperfections did not exist...."

The use of iodine vapor will impart iridescent blue, purple, and other colors to a coin's surface. This artificial surface is not well bonded to the metal, so a touch of acetone will remove it instantly (something which acetone will not do to natural iridescent toning; again, never use acetone without observing stringent safety precautions).

If a silver coin is exposed to an atmosphere containing sulfur fumes, over a period of weeks (or sooner if heat is applied, but this can be a dangerous process) it will take on a brownish or yellowish brown hue.

The iridescent surface most desired by collectors is in a way an artificial coloring, but one generated over a period of years. Beginning in the 1920s, it was popular to store or to house coins in cardboard holders covered with acetate slides. Such holders were made by M.L. Beistle in the 1920s, followed by Wayte Raymond's introduction of the "National" albums in the 1930s, followed still later by Meghrig, "Popular," "Library of Coins," and related products. Most later albums employed an inert plastic slide rather than acetate (the latter being highly inflammable). These cardboard albums contained sulfur. As years went by, the sulfur acted upon the edge of the coin, and then the flat surfaces, acting from the rim toward the center. Toning developed more intensely at the rims, lightening toward the center. The result over a period of time was a beautiful halo-like effect. Today, such toning is highly desired by collectors, and coins exhibiting this will often sell for premium prices.

This toning can be replicated or even accelerated by putting coins in old albums, but first dusting the interior of each hole (with the slides removed) lightly with sulfur. The coins are then put in the album, the slides reinserted, and then subjected to a warm atmosphere. It has been reported that after a period of a few weeks, attractive toning may result.

If you do nothing at all to a silver coin but simply leave it exposed to the atmosphere, within a few months, or certainly within a year or two, it will acquire a natural toning, probably brown with traces of yellow. This is caused by residual substances in the air, normal by-products from heating a home with natural gas, or from other combustion in the area.

We reiterate that cleaning a coin should be engaged in with great caution and forethought. For every single coin improved by cleaning, the values of many others have been lessened. It is better not to clean a coin than to clean it, be sorry, and then be faced with the complicated and uncertain task of retoning it acceptably!

Retoning Gold Coins

The surface of a gold coin changes slowly, and a piece which has been dipped to make it appear "brassy" will require many years to retone naturally. We are not aware of any comments in literature, or related to us by experimenters, concerning the satisfactory retoning of gold coins, except to say that it was once the practice of certain mints in the 19th century to "roast" gold coins before releasing them, thus giving them a deep golden color. We presume this same method would work today. We also presume it is more desirable to roast a gold coin at a relatively low temperature over a long period of time, than at a high temperature, for a high temperature may cause its own brand of damage to the piece and permanently discolor the surface.

Summary

Different methods have been employed with varying degrees of success for the retoning of copper, nickel, silver, and gold coins. No method is foolproof, and in any event a piece with natural toning as acquired over a period of years, is preferred by advanced collectors to a coin with artificial toning. While the purpose of the preceding essay on retoning coins is to restore to a level of acceptability coins which have been cleaned, a philosophy espoused by Dr. William H. Sheldon and others, readers should be aware that retoning is sometimes employed by unscrupulous sellers to disguise friction, hairlines, or surface defects. Further, such processes as chemical etching, whizzing, polishing, and other mechanical or chemical methods are sometimes employed, and then the results are masked by retoning. It is not possible for this or any other text to give all the variations of retoning, processing, whizzing, and other practices, and even if it were possible, probably something new would be invented tomorrow! Your best protection is to buy from a knowledgeable seller who guarantees the items sold. If you are in doubt concerning the appearance of a coin, by all means have it checked by experts before making a final purchase decision.

Chapter 12

Counterfeit Coins

Counterfeits exist in many fields: art, rare stamps, manuscripts, antiquities, and even stock certificates. Coins are no exception. Fortunately, stringent laws against counterfeiting United States coins have kept the abuse to a minimum.

This chapter discusses several different processes whereby counterfeit and altered coins are produced. The art of counterfeiting has reached a high level of sophistication, so in any event when you purchase a coin, insist upon a written receipt for it. Title cannot legally pass on a counterfeit coin, and if you later discover a piece to be counterfeit, and you have proof of purchase you stand an excellent chance of retrieving your investment. Otherwise, you are out of luck.

On numerous occasions while traveling around the world, the writer has seen scarce American $1, $3, and other pieces for sale. Upon examination, many of these turned out to be counterfeits, and in some countries, the majority of scarce dates offered in this manner have been counterfeits! In the United States, the owners of antique stores, flea markets, and the like have often sold counterfeit coins, perhaps unwittingly, for the average antique dealer, with such a wide area of endeavor to engage in, can hardly be expected to be a numismatic expert. However, from the standpoint of the buyer, it is important to realize that coins sold by others than professional numismatists should be examined with a special degree of care. We are not suggesting that the attempt at deception is deliberate, for in many if not most instances we are sure it is not, but the net effect is the same: a buyer purchasing a counterfeit coin has a worthless item.

Those deliberately selling counterfeit coins are very clever and often seek to prey upon such motivations on the part of the buyer as tax avoidance and bargain hunting.

In California, a wealthy doctor was induced into parting with a large sum of cash under the following circumstances. The coin seller was an antique dealer who told the prospective buyer something like this:

> "I do not know much about coins, but I do have a customer who has a tax problem. He is in a high income tax bracket, and he wants to sell his valuable coin collection, but only for cash — paper money — no checks, no invoices. According to what I read in the catalogues, this collection is worth about $100,000, but for cash it can be bought for $50,000. There are a lot of rare three-dollar gold coins in it and many other desirable things."

The doctor took the bait and arranged to visit the antique dealer for a private showing of the collection. The coins were brought out, and sure enough there were many scarce date three-dollar gold pieces, gold dollars, and even an MCMVII High Relief $20. And, sure enough, the coins had a catalogue value in excess of $100,000. All along, the antique dealer told the prospective buyer that he was simply the middleman, that he knew nothing about coins, and was serving simply to bring the owner of the coins together with a buyer, for which he was to receive a small fee.

Convinced he was getting a bargain, the doctor made an appointment to return later with $50,000 in cash. This was done, and the doctor took his bargain purchase home. All went well for several years. Then, he visited a leading Los Angeles coin dealer to investigate selling the coins, perhaps at auction or perhaps at outright sale. It took no more than a few minutes for the dealer to tell the doctor that nearly all the coins he purchased were forgeries. Each one was a diestruck counterfeit of excellent quality.

The doctor went back to the antique dealer, who still happened to be in business, but who professed only a dim recollection of the coin transaction a few years earlier, stating that he remembered it faintly, and earned a small commission at the time, but didn't remember who the coin seller was. The doctor, afraid of the legal consequences of what might appear to be tax evasion, elected not to pursue the matter further, and went off with his phony coins to lick his wounds.

If anyone ever attempts to sell you coins, but says that for various reasons he or she does not want to issue a receipt, our advice is to decline the purchase. You may be turning down a real bargain, but chances are excellent that there will be problems further down the line. Insist upon a receipt. Or, if the seller is willing, ask to have the coins certified by the American Numismatic Association Certification Service or the International Numismatic Society. For a fee, they will render an opinion concerning the authenticity of pieces submitted. Write in advance for a schedule of fees and also for a submission form.

In the paragraphs to follow we outline some of the types of counterfeits and alterations in existence. This discussion of the methods involved is not to encourage anyone to experiment in this regard, for the alteration and counterfeiting of coins is a criminal offense! However, by understanding the processes you will be able to identify certain types of spurious coins.

Alterations

Altered coins are genuine pieces, made at an official mint, but which have been altered to resemble something else. The presence or absence of a mintmark can often affect a coin's value greatly. For example, a 1916 Mercury dime from the Philadelphia Mint, without a mintmark, catalogued for $8 in EF-40 grade in *A Guide Book of United States Coins* in 1988. At the same time, a 1916-D Mercury dime, struck at the Denver Mint and with a tiny D mintmark on the reverse, catalogued in the same grade for $1,400, or over 150 times as much! This differential has resulted in widespread alteration of 1916 Philadelphia Mint Mercury dimes to give them the appearance of the prized 1916-D issue. In its most common form, the alteration consists of adding a D mintmark to the reverse, by solder or even glue. The D mintmark is usually obtained by cutting or grinding a genuine D mintmark from a later Mercury dime of low value, an issue in the 1940s for example.

Another popular forgery is the 1893-S silver dollar. Genuine specimens of the 1893 San Francisco Mint Morgan dollar catalogue for $3,250 in EF-40 grade, whereas an 1893 Philadelphia Mint (without mintmark) issue catalogues for just $100. Numerous alterations have been made by taking an S mintmark from a lower value Morgan silver dollar (such as a common 1881-S) and affixing it to the reverse of an 1893 Philadelphia issue, thus creating what seems to be an 1893-S.

Other popular mintmark additions include adding an S to the obverse of a 1909 V.D.B. Lincoln cent to create a prized 1909-S V.D.B., and adding a D mintmark to a 1914 Philadelphia Lincoln cent to create a rare 1914-D. Numerous other examples could be cited. In general, it pays to beware if a coin has a high value based upon the presence of a mintmark, especially in an instance in which other coins of the same date exist but are common. These common coins can be altered to resemble rare ones.

As a quick test for an added mintmark, subject the mintmark of the coin to high magnification. A stereo microscope, such as those employed by jewelers and rare coin dealers, is ideal, for it gives a three dimensional view. On the genuine, a mintmark under magnification will be an integral part of the coin's surface, with the edges of the mintmark smoothly blending into the flat area of the coin's surface at the junction points. On an alteration, sometimes crevices can be seen between the mintmark and the coin's surface, and in other instances the vertical edges of the added mintmark meet the surface of the coin at a sharp angle, rather than a curved or blended surface. Examine several common coins with mint-marks, and soon you will know what a genuine mintmark looks like. Then, if you see a falsely added one, you will notice the difference.

In addition, each die used to strike a coin has its own characteristics. Tiny die lines, finishing marks, die breaks, and other characteristics serve to "fingerprint" a die so that it is different from any others, even others used to strike the same date and mintmark variety. As the mintmarks are punched into the die by hand, mintmarks on different dies have different positions, sometime differing only microscopically, but still differing. The American Numismatic Association has published a series of guides giving the die characteristics of genuine specimens of certain widely altered and counterfeited coins. Such guides are useful in making a final determination.

A more sophisticated way to add a mintmark to a coin is to make a shell of the obverse of the coin, for example, then inset another reverse into it. In such an instance, an 1893 Philadelphia Mint silver dollar would be hollowed out from the back side, on a jeweler's lathe. Then from a common date San Francisco Mint dollar, perhaps an 1881-S, a disk would be cut, encompassing the entire reverse of the common silver dollar including the area bearing the mintmark. The reverse disk would then be inset into the obverse 1893 shell, then fastened together by use of silver solder. The seam, which is along the rim, can be obliterated by burnishing and filing. The result is what appears to be an 1893-S dollar. This same general method of creating a shell and inserting a part of another coin is commonly employed to create so-called magicians' tokens, available at novelty shops. Perhaps you have seen a two-headed Kennedy half dollar, for example, made as a magician's token.

There are several ways to detect such forgeries. Often (but not always) the fastening of two pieces of metal together will prevent the coin from having a sharp "ring." Balance the coin on the tip of your index finger (if the coin is in high grade, separate the coin from your finger by a glove or a piece of tissue paper). Lightly tap the coin on the edge, using another coin. The result should be a pronounced and lingering "ring," a bell-like tone. If you hear a click, rather than a lingering ring, be careful.

The weight of an alteration of this type is apt to differ from a genuine coin. Continuing the discussion of the example of the 1893-S Morgan dollar, an authentic specimen has a statutory weight of 412 1/2 grains. Allowing for wear and some slight differences in minting, an authentic specimen in close to Uncirculated grade should weigh fairly close to the standard. A coin weighing more, say 415 grains or higher, is automatically suspect, as is a coin weighing significantly less, say below 400 grains.

Still another method, and actually the best one, is to study the die characteristics of the 1893-S dollar, comparing your specimen with the die characteristics of a known genuine example.

In some instances, a coin without a mintmark is more valuable than a piece with a mintmark. Among Morgan silver dollars, the 1895 Philadelphia Mint dollar, without a mintmark, is considerably more valuable than an 1895-O or 1895-S issue. Over the years, many alterations have been made by removing O and S mintmarks to create what seem to be 1895 Philadelphia coins.

In the field of $20 gold pieces, the 1885 Philadelphia Mint issue, without a mintmark, is a great rarity and in AU-50 grade catalogued $12,500 in 1988. At the same time, an 1885-S (San Francisco) double eagle catalogued $600 in the same grade. Forgeries have been produced by removing S mintmarks from 1885-S coins, to create what seem to be 1885 Philadelphia coins.

Numerous examples of profitable mintmark removal can be cited. If a Philadelphia Mint issue of a coin is rare, and branch mint issues of the same year are common, watch for the possibility of mintmark removal.

The removal of a mintmark is best detected by examining the mintmark area under high magnification. If there seems to be scraping, rubbing, or other evidence of friction applied to this particular surface, particularly as compared with other surfaces of a coin, be careful. Sometimes traces of mintmark removal are obliterated by artificially wearing the entire coin (such as putting it in a tumbling machine of the type used by rock and mineral collectors), or by burnishing the entire coin, or by etching the surface, in which instances the evidence and mintmark removal may not be obvious.

The die characteristics of rare Philadelphia Mint coins have been recorded by the ANACS or the INS, so checking these die characteristics is the best test.

Another type of alteration involves changing the date of a coin. Years ago, a popular alteration was made by taking a 1944-D Lincoln cent and shaving or cutting away part of the first 4 numeral, thereby giving it the appearance of a 1 and creating a "1914-D" cent, a rare variety, from a common 1944-D cent. This variety is quickly spotted by the fact that the upright of the first 4, which was used to create the 1, was too far to the right and was not evenly spaced between the 9 and the final 4. However, beginners could be easily fooled. Numerous forgeries of 1913 Liberty Head nickels, one of America's greatest rarities, have been made by taking 1903 Liberty nickels, removing the 0, and soldering or otherwise affixing a 1 in its place, thus creating a "1913". Some 1893-S silver dollar forgeries have been made by taking 1883-S dollars, removing the second 8 and affixing a 9 in its place, thus creating an "1893-S."

During the 19th century a popular forgery was made by taking a 1798 large cent and retooling the last figure so it appeared to be "1799," a rare date. As authentic 1799 cents have specific die characteristics, such forgeries can be told by comparing the relative position of other die features. Also, numerous fake 1856 Flying Eagle cents, a rare date, have been made by altering the last digit in the date of a common 1858 Flying Eagle cent.

Electrotype and Cast Coins

Beginning in the 19th century, electrotype copies were made of many scarce dates. This was not viewed as illegal, and, among others, the British Museum and the American Numismatic Society each sold electrotype copies of colonial and other coins for study purposes. In other instances, individuals deliberately created electrotypes as a deception.

An electrotype is created by taking an authentic coin, say a 1799 large cent, and making separate obverse and reverse impressions by forcing the coin into soft wax. The coin is then removed, and the impression of each half is lightly coated with graphite, which is an electrically conductive substance. Each half is then immersed into a plating solution, and copper metal is electrodeposited. The result is a sharp impression of the obverse and, separately, the reverse, with the back of each impression being rough. The two separate impressions are removed from the wax mold, trimmed, and ground down. Then the two disks are soldered or otherwise put together. If the process is not continued beyond this point, a fine seam can be observed around the edge. However, in some instances this seam is obliterated by copper plating the entire finished production, or by burnishing or smoothing the edge.

Electrotype copies do not have a clear "ring" when balanced on your index finger and tapped lightly on the edge with another coin. Instead, they have a dull click. In addition, a typical electrotype is apt to be heavier than the prescribed standard.

Some electrotypes were made up as thin shells, brazed together, and then filled with lead to give them weight. Many scarce half cents, large cents, 1792 pattern coins, and colonial coins have been copied in this manner. Lead-filled electrotypes are seriously overweight and lack the prescribed "ring."

More sophisticated are cast forgeries. These became popular beginning in the 1930s, when centrifugal casting equipment became widely available in dental laboratories (for the making of bridges) and in jewelers' workshops (for casting rings, ornaments, and other jewelry).

A mold is prepared from a genuine coin, then the mold is centrifugally filled with gold, silver, or some other metal. The resultant coin will have the proper "ring" or sonority, but may have a slightly porous surface from the mold, and may not be of the correct weight. Also, the edge may show a spot where the "gate" to the mold was, although this spot can be removed by filing, tooling, or engraving.

Cast forgeries have all the characteristics of the coin used to make them. If the original coin has nicks and marks in certain positions, every cast of that coin will have the same nicks and marks in the same positions. By comparing multiple examples of known rarities, casts have been identified by having similar circulation marks. Again, the American Numismatic Association Certification Service has published information on certain known casts including identification marks. Casts can be extremely deceptive, so much that laboratory analysis is required. Again, we caution you never to buy coins "as is." Insist upon a written receipt.

Die-Struck Counterfeits

Beginning in the 1960s, a new method of die creation became known to numismatists. Designated as the spark erosion process, by this method a tracing point or finger traverses the surfaces of a genuine coin, an 1877 Indian cent for example, and by means of a pantagraph or tracing arm mechanism, a second finger creates a reverse impression of the original coin by etching a steel blank or die with a tiny electric spark. This process takes a long time, but the result is a faithful reproduction, in reverse on a die, of an original piece. Two dies, representing the obverse and reverse, are thus created, and are used to strike pieces on a coining press. Under magnification, coins struck from these dies are apt to show minute granularity, but polishing and finishing of the dies sometimes removes such traces. Spark erosion dies are a menace and since the 1960s have been an object of study. The spark erosion process cannot reproduce microscopic die details such as finishing lines, die scratches, and the like, so the identification of forgeries has often been by this route, again ANACS and INS.

Counterfeit dies can be made by impact. Just as high winds in a tornado can drive a straw into a telephone pole, a genuine coin, if projected with force at high speed against a piece of unhardened steel, will be driven into the steel and create an incuse impression of it, although with very slight distortion. This method is occasionally used to create counterfeit dies.

Still another method to create counterfeit dies is to take a genuine coin and trace it with a pantagraph point, adjusted to create a copy many times larger. The copy, which can be in plaster or another soft substance, is then smoothed, adjusted, and refined. Then by means of a reducing lathe, a die is created from this larger master. Such dies can be very deceptive, and the best way to identify coins struck from them is to compare microscopic die finishing lines and other characteristics.

A further way to create dies is by direct engraving. With engraving tools and letter and numeral punches, numerous false dies have been created. As the position of the die features is apt to vary from the originals, most counterfeits thus made will not fool numismatists, but they will often fool the general public. If such dies are made with great care, however, numismatists can be deceived. In the 19th century, one J.A. Bolen, a Massachusetts engraver, produced many very clever forgeries of colonial and early American coins by engraving new dies. Interestingly, these copies, which are identifiable by minor characteristics and sometimes by secret marks deliberately put on the dies, have become collectors' items in their own right and are in great demand today (although the price of these is much less than that commanded by originals).

Summary

We reiterate that your best protection against counterfeits is to buy from a knowledgeable seller, and obtain an invoice. In this way you have recourse if a piece is later proved to be false. Buying coins "for cash" and without invoices, has often led to great problems in the past, so we strongly recommend that you avoid this. We are not suggesting that antique dealers, flea market operators, and the like never have bargains for sale, for this is not the case. However, of the many counterfeit coins we have seen over the years (and we have acted as advisors to the Treasury Department, the American Numismatic Association, the Secret Service, and other agencies in this regard) most have been the result of "bargain hunting." Be careful at the outset. Lest anyone get the idea that in numismatics forgeries are a bigger problem than elsewhere, we again mention that in such fields as antiques, art, stamps, old cars, or just about any other collecting endeavor, such problems surface. If anything, the collector has greater protection in numismatics, for the counterfeiting of United States coins is a criminal offense, as is the intentional selling of them.

Chapter 13

Dictionary of Grading Terms

The following Dictionary of Grading Terms lists terms specifically identified with the grading of United States coins, and certain coin characteristics and areas which are closely identified with grading.

In some instances, the same word may have different or expanded definitions in areas other than grading, but such additional definitions are not germane here.

About Good. A well-worn coin, nearly smooth, with few features visible. Better than Fair but less than Good.

About Uncirculated. Grading term; always capitalized. Abbreviated as AU. Same as Almost Uncirculated. Describes a piece which is very close to Uncirculated or MS-60 grade, but which falls short of the mark because of friction or light wear. In the ANA grading scale the numbers AU-50, AU-55, and AU-58 describe ascending degrees of AU preservation.

abrasions. Scuffs, slide marks, or other marks on a coin made by moving contact between the coin and another coin, or the coin and a hard object or surface. Abrasions can occur on coins in various grades from the lowest to Uncirculated and Proof.

Accugrade. A system devised by Alan Hager and advertised widely beginning in the late 1980s, primarily for use in grading Morgan silver dollars.

acetone. A highly volatile solvent, available at drug stores and chemical suppliers, used to remove grease, dirt, and foreign material from the surface of a coin, without chemically altering the metallic structure of the surface itself (in other words, toning, lustre, and other surface metallic features are not changed). Acetone must be used in a well-ventilated area, away from spark or flame, and the fumes must not be inhaled.

adjectival grading. Grading by adjectival notations (as opposed to numerical grading). Adjectival descriptions, capitalized in numismatic usage, are used. Examples include Good, Very Good, Fine, Very Fine, Extremely Fine, About Uncirculated, Uncirculated, Choice Uncirculated, Choice Proof, etc.

adjustment marks. Marks made on the planchet at the Mint, to reduce the weight of the planchet so that it conforms with the statutory requirements. In the early days, especially the 1790s through the first several decades of the 19th century, it was a common practice to make copper and silver planchets slightly overweight. A large corps of women was kept busy weighing planchets on balance scales, and then drawing a metal file across the surface to remove excess weight. These file marks, a series of parallel grooves, can still be seen on many coins from this era. They are particularly visible in areas of higher relief on coins, including the rims, stars, obverse portrait, and reverse eagle.

aesthetic appeal. The artistic appeal which a coin has for the viewer. The desirability of a coin as evidenced by a combination of attractive toning or lustre, pleasing surface coloration, attractive planchet, and other artistic considerations. The aesthetic appeal of a given coin will vary from viewer to viewer, depending upon personal taste.

altered date, altered mintmark, alteration. The alteration of a date, mintmark, or other feature on a coin to give it the appearance of being a different issue. For example, the addition of a D mintmark to a 1916 Philadelphia Mint Mercury dime, to falsely give it the appearance of a 1916-D, is an alteration. The removal of the S mintmark from an 1885-S double eagle to give the coin the appearance of an 1885 Philadelphia Mint issue (which has no mintmark) is another example. Alterations are performed in different ways. There is the addition or removal of numerals and mintmarks, or the changing of one number into another by engraving or adding metal, changing the last 8 in an 1858 Flying Eagle cent, a common date, to resemble a 6, to appear as a rare 1856 Flying Eagle cent.

aluminum. A metal used for pattern coinage during the late 19th century. In addition, impressions of dies of certain Proof coins were made in aluminum. At the time, thought was given to aluminum for coinage, but after experimentation, no commercial production ensued. In 1974, the mint experimented with aluminum as a substitute for copper in cents, and several pattern strikings were made. Aluminum tends to show marks easily, and even light mishandling will give an aluminum coin a scuffed appearance. Within a short time, a natural oxidation or toning occurs on the surface of aluminum coins, giving the pieces a pleasing light gray appearance.

American Numismatic Association. An association of coin collectors formed in 1891 to promote the artistic and scientific aspects of numismatics. Publishers of *The Numismatist*, a monthly journal. This non-profit group has its headquarters at 818 North Cascade Avenue, Colorado Springs, Colorado 80903, and in 1988 had roughly 30,000 members on its roster. The American Numismatic Association, usually abbreviated as ANA, also operates the American Numismatic Association Certification Service.

American Numismatic Association Certification Service. Formed in the 1970s under the direction of Virgil Hancock, Abe Kosoff, John Jay Pittman, and others, this department of the American Numismatic Association maintains a laboratory for the authentication and evaluation of rare coins for a fee. For genuine coins, a certificate giving an opinion of authenticity is issued.

American Numismatic Association Grading Standards. A system of grading coins, formulated in 1976 by Kenneth E. Bressett and Abe Kosoff, and outlined in a book, *The Official American Numismatic Association Grading Standards for United States Coins*, subsequently expanded and updated, with the third edition issued in 1987. The introduction to all three editions is by Q. David Bowers. An adaptation of the Sheldon Scale, the ANA grading standards are based on numbers from About Good-3 (abbreviated as AG-3) to MS-70, the former coin being very worn and the latter being in perfect Mint State. As of 1987, the ANA grading standards consisted of the following: About Good-3 (AG-3), Good-4 (G-4), Very Good-8 (VG-8), Fine-12 (F-12), Very Fine-20 (VF-20), Choice Very Fine-30 (VF-30), Extremely Fine-40

(EF-40), Choice Extremely Fine-45 (EF-45), About Uncirculated-50 (AU-50), Choice About Uncirculated-55 (AU-55), Very Choice About Uncirculated-58 (AU-58; a "new" grade added in 1987); and 11 degrees of Uncirculated, from MS-60 to MS-70 inclusive.

ANACS Grading Service. Formed in the late 1970s, the American Numismatic Association Grading Service was operated by the American Numismatic Association Certification Service. In 1990 it was sold to Amos Press and for a fee, renders an opinion concerning the grade of a coin.

artificial toning. Surface coloration, oxidation, tarnish, patination, toning—many adjectives can be used—applied to a coin artificially, over a short period of time, by chemicals, heat, or exposure to fumes (as contrasted to natural toning, or toning acquired by a coin in the atmosphere over a period of many months to many years).

bagmarks. Nicks, scuffs, abrasions, and other contact marks which a coin has acquired by coin-to-coin contact in a mint or bank bag. Such marks can also be acquired during the minting process (see page 215). In general, coins of heavier weight and in softer metals are more prone to acquiring bagmarks. The fewer bagmarks a coin has, the higher the degree of quality assigned to it in the Uncirculated or Proof range. Thus, a coin with very few bagmarks can be MS-65 or finer, but a heavily bagmarked coin may be MS-60. There are many intermediate variations.

beaded border, beading. A circle of beads around the rim of a coin, or near the rim, serving as a decorative or protective border, as used on the 1793 Liberty Cap cent, the obverse of the Standing Liberty quarter, the 1918 Illinois centennial commemorative half dollar, and others. Some beads are circular and others are pellet-shaped.

borderline Uncirculated. A term in use prior to the widespread adoption of numerical grading in the late 1970s, which refers to a coin which is close to Uncirculated but not quite. Today, such pieces are described as AU-55 or AU-58. Also see cabinet friction.

brilliant. Adjective used to modify a grade, such as brilliant Uncirculated, brilliant Proof, etc., denoting that the coin has bright (rather than toned or oxidized) surfaces. From the 1950s through the late 1970s, in the years before numerical grading became widespread, brilliant often signified a coin of superior quality. Thus, a coin described simply as Uncirculated was an "ordinary" Uncirculated coin, whereas a brilliant Uncirculated specimen was considered to be a selected example. This led to the "brilliant is best" syndrome, so that many collectors cleaned their coins to make them appear bright.

brilliant Proof. A Proof coin with brilliant surfaces.

brilliant Uncirculated. An Uncirculated or Mint State coin with brilliant surfaces.

bronze. An alloy consisting of 95% copper and 5% tin and zinc, popularized in France in the early 1860s, and first used on a widespread basis in the United States as a metal for privately issued tokens during the Civil War. Mint officials adopted the metal for United States coinage commencing with the bronze Indian cent of 1864 and the two-cent piece of the same year. From then to 1982 bronze was a staple metal for cent coinage (with several alloy variations over the years). Commonly, copper is used as a synonym for bronze, although bronze is the technically correct term.

Brown and Dunn. Martin R. Brown and John W. Dunn produced *A Guide to the Grading of United States Coins*, first published in 1958 and issued in several editions after that, by the Whitman Publishing Company. From 1958 until the advent of *Photograde* by James F. Ruddy, in 1970, the Brown and Dunn reference was the only popular guide to United States coin grading. At the time, vendors would often state "grading by Brown and Dunn."

brushed. Descriptive of a coin which has had its surfaces rubbed with a brush or cloth, and which shows hairlines or tiny parallel scratches as a result, a negative situation. On the other hand, brushing of copper coins with a jeweler's camel hair brush, a process which removes verdigris and which does not leave tiny scratches, is considered to be desirable by numismatists.

burnished. Polished, usually with an engraving tool or motorized wheel, to remove portions of a coin's surface, and in the process to remove scratches, initials, or other marks, sometimes leaving a telltale depression in the coin. Burnishing must always be indicated as part of a coin's description.

business strike. A term, popularized by the New Netherlands Coin Company in the 1950s, and widely adopted since that time, which refers to a coin minted for circulation and commerce (as opposed to a Proof coin minted especially for collectors).

cabinet friction. A term popular for many years, but which fell out of use with the advent of widespread numerical grading in the late 1970s. The term refers to rubbing marks or friction marks on the high spots of a coin, fancifully or hopefully described as having been acquired by movement of the coins in a drawer in a collector's wooden cabinet (the primary way in which coins were stored until the 1930s). It was intended that the cabinet friction term would be a gentler description for rubbing or the light effects of short-term circulation. Thus, a coin years ago might have been described as "Uncirculated with light cabinet friction." Today, the same term is replaced by AU-55 or AU-58. Also see borderline Uncirculated.

cameo, cameolike. A term used to describe a coin of which the central device or portrait is frosted or has a satiny or other non-mirror-like surface, and which is set against a field which is prooflike or Proof, thus highlighting the central portrait. In other instances, a coin which has a small portrait surrounded by a large field can be described as having a cameo appearance regardless of grade; the half cent obverse design of 1795 being an example.

carbon spot. An oxidation spot or area, usually black, which forms on the surface of a copper, bronze, or nickel coin (occasionally other metals as well) as a result of dampness or moisture. Tiny carbon spots are sometimes referred to as carbon flecks or carbon specks.

cartwheel lustre. Frosty mint lustre or brilliance, as found on a business strike coin, which, when held at an angle to the light and turned slowly, gives a moving "cartwheel" effect. This type of lustre is often seen on Morgan silver dollars and other coins with large surfaces.

centering. Descriptive of the position of the planchet in relation to the dies. A well-centered coin is one in which the planchet was placed in the center between the dies, so that the border or rim is of equal width and definition in all areas. Coins which are not centered are described as being off center.

certification. Descriptive of the process in which an individual, firm, organization, or other entity examines a coin and issues a certificate giving an opinion of the authenticity, grade, or other characteristics.

choice. An adjective which signifies that a coin is one of the better examples of its class. Capitalized when used with a specific grading term, such as Choice Extremely Fine, Choice Uncirculated, Choice Proof, etc.

Choice About Uncirculated. Descriptive of a high-grade About Uncirculated coin, a piece which on the numerical grading scale is designated as AU-55.

Choice Extremely Fine. Descriptive of a select or exceptional Extremely Fine coin, designated as EF-45 on the numerical grading scale.

Choice Proof. An exceptional Proof coin with few marks or defects, a grade which prior to 1987 the ANA grading standards defined as Proof-65. In 1987 the Choice Proof designation was discontinued by the ANA.

Choice Uncirculated. Descriptive of an outstanding Uncirculated coin, one with few defects or problems. Until the third edition of *Official ANA Grading Standards of United States Coins* was published in 1987, Choice Uncirculated equated to MS-65 on the ANA grading scale, although in the coin market many buyers and sellers use the term to describe MS-63. Perhaps to end this double standard, the ANA dropped the description in 1987.

Choice Very Fine. Descriptive of an outstanding Very Fine coin, equal to VF-30 on the ANA grading scale.

clash mark. Usually plural, clash marks. Descriptive of outlines and traces of designs seen in the field of a coin, and caused by die damage occurring when two dies come together without an intervening planchet. This causes certain obverse die designs and images to be transferred to the reverse die, and vice versa, so that coins later struck from these dies show evidence of the design transfer. Clash marks are seen on many different denominations of coins but are particularly prevalent on various issues of the Philadelphia Mint struck prior to the advent of steam-powered coinage in 1836. Small-diameter coins of later years, especially silver three-cent pieces and half dimes of the 1850s and 1860s, often show clash marks.

cleaning. The process of treating a coin to remove dirt, verdigris, and sediment from the surfaces, a procedure which can be beneficial. More often the term is used to refer to the application of chemical or abrasive agents to a coin, to remove toning or to change the coloration of the surface, a situation which is often undesirable (refer to Chapter 9 on cleaning in the present book).

collar. A device used in a coining press to restrict the flow of metal outward from the dies. When a coin is struck by the dies, the metal flows toward the edges and is stopped by the collar. If the collar has a decorative or geometric design, that design will be formed on the edge of a coin. Thus, a reeded collar will create a reeded edge on a coin, and a collar with lettering (such as used on Saint-Gaudens $20 pieces struck from 1907-1933) will transfer appropriate lettering to the piece.

color, coloration. Descriptive of the hues or color characteristics of a coin's surface. Thus, a large cent can have a reddish-brown coloration, a silver dollar can have an iridescent coloration, etc.

copper. A basic elemental metal used in the production of United States half cents, large cents, certain pattern coins, and other series, especially tokens, medals, and store cards, mainly before the mid 1860s, after which the use of copper was largely replaced in coinage by bronze, an alloy containing copper (see bronze).

copper-nickel. An alloy used to produce Flying Eagle cents 1856-1858 and certain Indian cents 1859-1864, consisting of 88 parts copper and 12 parts nickel. The alloy has a yellowish appearance.

counterfeit. Descriptive of a false coin. A piece which has been cast, electrolytically reproduced, or struck from false dies, in imitation of a genuine piece.

counterstamp. A punch, hallmark, or other device applied after minting to the surface of a coin, for the purpose of creating an advertisement, identifying its origin, changing its value, or simply as a whim by someone possessing punches. Many United States coins were counterstamped, primarily by private individuals, but occasionally by the government (as in the instance of the 1848 quarter eagles counter-stamped with CAL. on the reverse, to signify that they were struck from gold obtained from California.)

denticles. Toothlike projections extending from the rim of a coin toward the center.

detail, details. Descriptive of fine characteristics of a coin's design, including the hair of Miss Liberty, the serifs on letters, leaves in a wreath, and other small details of a portrait, motif, or overall design

die. A metal cylinder on the end of which have been impressed or engraved the incuse features of a typical coin. Used in pairs, one with an obverse design and the other with a reverse design, to strike coins by impressing the designs on a planchet inserted between the dies.

die lines. A series of lines in the die, which are transferred to create raised lines in the field or other area of a coin. Common on business strike coinage in instances in which the dies were not polished to remove the lines. An important consideration for grading, for die lines have no adverse effect on the grade of a coin. Die lines are sometimes confused with hairlines, the latter being minute scratches in a coin applied after the coin was struck.

die striations, die striae. A series of parallel raised ridges on a coin caused by metal flowing into lines in the die. These die lines were caused by a file, grinding wheel, or other abrasive instrument used to remove burrs from the die surface and to render the die fit for coinage. Such marks have no adverse affect on the value of a coin, but must not be confused with hairlines which do have an adverse affect.

diebreak. A raised irregular ridge on a coin, usually extending from the rim toward the center, which results from the metal coining die having a crack. The metal in the planchet is forced into the crack thus producing the diebreak.

dipping. The process of immersing a coin in a cleaning solution to remove toning or oxidation and thereby changing the color or general appearance of the coin's surface. For more information refer to Chapter 10 on cleaning in this book.

doubled die. Describes a coin struck from a die which shows certain lettering or other features slightly doubled. This effect was caused by impressing the master or hub die into the coining die, and then impressing the master or hub die again, but in a slightly different alignment, to cause doubling. The most famous issue is the 1955 Doubled Die Lincoln cent.

Extremely Fine. A coin grade, capitalized in this usage, describing a coin which has but light effects of circulation (refer to detailed description elsewhere). In the numerical grading scale it is described as EF-40 and EF-45.

Fair. A grading term, capitalized, describing a piece which is worn nearly smooth. In the numerical scale sometimes described as Fair-2 (never abbreviated as F-2, for the abbreviation F is reserved for Fine).

field. The flat surface of a coin, the background, against which the stars, lettering, portrait, and other features are set.

Fine. A grading term, capitalized, indicative of a coin which has seen extensive wear but which still contains nearly all its lettering and prominent design features. In the ANA grading system designated as Fine-12, abbreviated as F-12. On the Sheldon Scale, Fine-12 or Fine-15, the latter being a slightly nicer coin.

flan. A term, primarily of European usage, designating a coin planchet or blank disk.

flat strike. Descriptive of a coin which has been struck in a manner in which certain design elements, particularly those in the highest areas of relief, are poorly defined. This is usually caused by the dies being separated slightly too far apart, so that the metal is not forced into the deepest recesses of the die. Flat strikes are common in United States coinage and in certain areas are the rule, not the exception, such areas including branch mint Buffalo nickels, Standing Liberty quarters, and Liberty Walking half dollars of the 1920s.

frost, frosted. Frost, often mint frost, describes the lustre on a coin, the flashing or cartwheel graininess which the surface of an Uncirculated coin displays when held in the light.

gem. A non-specific term referring to a coin, usually Uncirculated or Proof, which has very few defects and which is among the finest of its kind. Capitalized in combination with a grading term, such as Gem Uncirculated and Gem Proof. Prior to 1987, Gem Uncirculated in the ANA grading scale referred to a coin in MS-67 condition, and Gem Proof referred to a Proof-67 example, but in 1987 the use of the Gem term was discontinued.

gold. An elemental coinage metal used in the production of high-denomination United States coins, from gold dollars to double eagles, plus commemorative and private $50 pieces. In coinage, nine parts of gold are typically alloyed with one part of copper, the copper adding strength.

Good. A grading term, capitalized, which refers to a coin showing a high degree of wear but for which the date and most lettering are still readable. In the numerical system, Good-4 and Good-6 are used, abbreviated as G-4 and G-6. Refer to the specific definition of this grade elsewhere in the present book.

grading service. A commercial service, either for profit or operated by a nonprofit organization, set up in business to grade coins for a fee and to issue a certificate stating the findings. In practice, the findings of various grading services often differ greatly from each other.

granularity, granular surface. Descriptive of porosity or minutely irregular surfaces caused by oxidation or by striking on a planchet with a rough or regular surface. Typically, granularity is seen on early copper coins.

guaranteed grade. A merchandising term in which a seller states that the grade is guaranteed to be at a certain level. Guaranteed grades were a popular promotional device until the mid 1980s, when the American Numismatic Association changed the interpretation of its own grading standards, resulting in the situation in which coins guaranteed by sellers earlier were found to fall short of later ANA grading evaluations.

hairlines. Descriptive of tiny lines or scratches in the surface of a coin, usually the result of cleaning with an abrasive.

high relief. A design feature which is raised on the surface of a coin to an exceptional degree. The best known example is the MCMVII High Relief Saint-Gaudens $20, made in 1907, which has a sculptured appearance. The high relief caused great problems in striking, for multiple blows of the coining press were required to bring the design up properly. Later, the high relief feature was modified to a shallow format to permit highspeed production.

holed. A coin which has been pierced for suspension on a bracelet or for some other purpose. Some holed coins have been carefully plugged or repaired so that close examination is required to determine that they were holed earlier. A hole in a coin, whether or not it has been repaired, must always be described.

impaired Proof. A Proof coin which has seen extensive handling or which has evidence of light circulation and is thus less than Proof-60 on the numerical scale. An impaired Proof coin is best described as Proof-50 or Proof-55, if areas of the Proof surface are still visible. Since Proof coins are never Uncirculated to begin with — Uncirculated being a term pertaining to business strikes — a lightly worn Proof cannot be About Uncirculated (AU). A Proof coin worn below Proof-50 can be described in the manner of any other coin, such as VF-30, EF-40, and so on. If some traces of the Proof surface are still visible, then a description such as "EF-40, struck as a Proof but now with evidence of circulation," may be appropriate.

incuse. The opposite of relief, a coin design which is recessed in the field of a coin, rather than raised. United States quarter eagles and half eagles 1908-1929 are of the incuse format.

International Numismatic Service. A private authentication and grading service which, for a fee, will evaluate coins and issue an opinion concerning them.

iridescence. Multicolored rainbow-like toning on a coin, particularly a silver coin.

lamination, planchet lamination. Descriptive of a flaking or peeling of metal from the surface of a coin, caused by incomplete bonding of metal in the original planchet.

lettered edge. An edge which bears a lettered inscription. Examples in United State coinage include half cents of the 1790s, large cents 1793-1795, half dollars 1794-1836, silver dollars 1794-1804, and $20 pieces 1907-1933. Early coins had the lettering applied to the planchet separately before striking. The lettering on the edge of the 1907-1933 $20 pieces was produced by a collar at the time the coins were struck.

light strike. Descriptive of a coin which has certain areas, particularly those in relief, lightly or poorly defined. The same as weak strike.

lint mark. An incuse mark on a coin resulting from a piece of lint, thread, human hair, particle, or other substance adhering to the surface of a die, the image of which is transferred to coins struck from that die. Lint marks are especially prevalent on Proof coins of the 1850s and 1860s and result from lint left by cleaning rags used to wipe the dies at periodic intervals. As lint marks were produced at the time of striking, they do not have the negative connotation that scratches and other marks produced at a later time have, but lint marks are not desirable, and extensive lint marks or particularly prominent ones should be a part of a coin's grading description.

mark, marks. Evidences of a coin having come into contact with another coin, a hard surface, or some other object. Marks can take many forms and include nicks, gouges, scratches, abrasions, hairlines, etc.

market price, market value. The generally accepted price or value which a coin in a specific grade, and with specific surface characteristics, will change hands on a retail basis between two knowledgeable buyers.

Matte Proof. Descriptive of a special Proof process, capitalized when used. The Matte Proof finish was popularized at the Paris Mint in the 1890s and was used at the Philadelphia Mint to produce coins for collectors beginning in the first decade of the 20th century. Lincoln cents 1909-1916, Buffalo nickels 1913-1916, quarter eagles 1908-1915, half eagles 1908-1915, and Saint-Gaudens double eagles 1907-1915 have this finish. Matte Proofs were made by pickling the dies, or otherwise treating them, to give them an etched surface. Coins struck from such dies have a grainy or satinlike finish, quite unlike the mint frost which characterizes business strikes. Several variations, generally grouped under the Matte Proof term, were used, especially on gold coins, and include Roman Finish Proofs, Sandblast Proofs, and Satin Proofs. Matte Proofs were not popular with collectors and contributed to the discontinuation of Proof coinage in 1916.

milled edge, milling. Technically a term which is descriptive of the raised rim around the outside obverse and reverse border of a coin, but in popular usage descriptive of the vertical reeding on a coin's edge.

mint. An establishment specializing in the production of coinage.

mint lustre. The grainy frost characteristic of an Uncirculated business strike coin. The frost can be brilliant, as struck, or can exhibit toning.

Mint State. A grading term, capitalized, which refers to an Uncirculated coin, or a coin which has never been placed into commercial circulation. Depending upon the number of bag marks and surface contact indications, on the Sheldon and ANA grading scales, a Mint State coin can range from MS-60, or basic Uncirculated, a coin with many contact marks, to MS-70, or a perfect example with not a single mark. In 1986, the American Numismatic Association Board of Governors adopted the use of 11 different Mint State designations, comprising each number from MS-60 through and including MS-70.

minting, minting process. The procedure by which coins are struck.

natural toning. Surface coloration, oxidation, or patination of a coin due to normal exposure to atmospheric conditions over a long period of time. A synonym for tarnish, but as tarnish has a pejorative connotation, the toning term is preferred. Compare to artificial toning.

nick, nicks. Surface marks or indentations on a coin resulting from momentary contact with a sharp object or another coin. When jumbled together in a mint bag, coins typically acquire many nicks as a result of contact with each other.

nickel, nickel alloy. The nickel term is used to describe three-cent pieces of the 1865-1889 years and five-cent pieces beginning with the Shield type in 1866 and minted to present times. It consists of an alloy composed of 75 parts copper and 25 parts nickel, but having a silvery surface more characteristic of nickel than of copper.

numerical grading. The use of numbers in connection with grading, as proposed by Dr. William H. Sheldon in 1949, and later revised by others, including the American Numismatic Association. In the numerical grading system, a Mint State or Uncirculated coin, for example, is described with a number in addition to the general description or abbreviation, as MS-60, MS-65, etc. Numerical grading is used by many as a replacement for adjectival grading.

Numismatic Certification Institute. A private service, which for a fee will render an opinion concerning the grade of a coin.

Numismatic Guaranty Corporation. A private service, which for a fee, will render an opinion concerning the grade of a coin.

obverse. The front of a coin. Usually, but not always, the side bearing the portrait and/or date. Among commemorative coins in particular there are many exceptions to this general rule. In popular parlance, the "head" side of a coin.

off center. A coin whose planchet was not properly centered at the time of striking, and which now has the devices improperly centered, resulting in the rim or border being prominent on one side and small or nonexistent on the other.

Official ANA Grading Standards for United States Coins. The proper name for the book outlining the numerical grading system used by the American Numismatic Association, usually referred to simply as the ANA grading system.

original. A coin which was struck from official dies at the time indicated by the date on the coin. Compare with restrike, a coin issued from official dies but at a later date.

overdate. A date which in the die is punched over an earlier date, such as 1807/6 (1807 over 6). This procedure was used as an economy measure. A leftover or unused die from an earlier date was overpunched with a later current date and used for coinage. Under magnification, traces of the earlier date can be seen. Many different overdates occur throughout United States coinage.

overgrading. The practice, intentional or otherwise, of assigning a higher grade to a coin than the coin merits.

oxidation. Corrosion, spotting, or other discoloration on a coin's surface as a result of chemical action of the surface with the atmosphere.

patina. Toning on a coin. A positive term usually employed to describe natural toning which is pleasing in appearance.

Photograde. A photographic guide to the grading of United States coins, written by James F. Ruddy and first published in 1970, subsequently selling to the extent of hundreds of thousands of copies and earning recognition as the most popular grading guide ever produced; the book you are now reading.

planchet. A blank circular disk of copper, bronze, nickel alloy, silver, or some other metal from which a coin is made.

planchet defect. A fissure, area of missing metal, or other indications on a finished coin that the planchet struck was defective.

platinum. A precious metal not used for American coinage production, but experimented with at the Philadelphia Mint during the 19th century. Used to produce certain coins of other countries (for example, certain Russian coins of the 1830s were struck in platinum).

plugged. A coin which was holed or pierced and subsequently repaired by having the hole filled. A plugged coin must be so noted as part of a grading description.

polished. Descriptive of a coin which has had a mirror-like surface applied after striking, by use of jeweler's rouge, a buffing wheel, silver polish, or some other abrasive agent. A coin which has been polished must be so noted as part of the grading description.

polyvinyl chloride, PVC. A plasticizer used as part of certain transparent flexible coin holders which after a period of time deposits a greasy substance or goo on the surface of a coin, which in the instance of copper, bronze, and nickel alloy coins can permanently change the coloration and character of the coin's surface. PVC-content coin holders should not be used for long-term storage and should be replaced by holders made of inert substances. PVC-content holders were very popular in numismatics until the early 1980s, when the deleterious effects were first recognized.

Poor. A grading term, capitalized, signifying a coin which is in the lowest possible condition, a piece worn nearly completely smooth and barely identifiable as to general type. Sometimes noted as Poor-1 (never abbreviated as P-1, however, as this may be confused with Proof).

porosity. A characteristic of a coin's surface resulting in a fine etching or granularity, the result of oxidation after the coin was struck, or in some instances the result of striking on a granular planchet. Most often seen among early copper issues in the United States series.

portrait. A head, bust, or other representation of a person used as part of a coin design.

presentation piece. A coin which was carefully struck, either a business strike or a Proof, but which was intended for numismatic or presentation purposes.

processed coin, processing. Describes a coin which has had its surface artificially treated by a chemical, abrasion, or some other method in an effort to make it appear as a grade higher than it really is. Types of processing include whizzing, burnishing, and polishing. In a coin description, evidences of processing must be noted.

Professional Coin Grading Service. A service set up by a group of rare coin dealers in 1986, which for a fee will render a grading opinion. Coins certified by the Professional Coin Grading Service, often abbreviated as PCGS, are encased in sonically sealed plastic holders popularly referred to as "slabs."

problem coin. A slang term referring to a coin which is not readily saleable due to poor striking, cleaning, or some other problem; a piece which therefore must be sold at a sharp discount from the price merited by unimpaired examples of the same technical grade.

Proof. A term, capitalized in numismatic usage, referring to a special surface of mirror-like quality given to the fields of a coin. Proofs are struck from dies whose fields have been polished to a high mirror-like degree. Most Proofs over the years have been struck on carefully prepared planchets of excellent quality, and have been produced on slow-speed presses to bring up all the design elements carefully. However, there are exceptions, and certain Proofs are carelessly struck, and still others (such as many 1878 Shield nickels) resemble business strikes. See separate discussion on Proof coins in the present text. In the numerical grading system a number is given after the Proof term to designate its quality. Proofs which have not seen circulation are arranged from Proof-60, or a coin with extensive hairlines or contact marks, to Proof-70, a perfect coin. Proofs which have seen circulation and wear are described in lesser grades, such as Proof-50, Proof-55, etc. A worn Proof can never be described as "About Uncirculated," for a Proof coin is different from an Uncirculated coin and was never "Uncirculated" to begin with.

prooflike. A term, not capitalized in usage, referring to a mirror-like surface on a coin, but on a piece which was not intentionally struck as a Proof, although a prooflike coin can exhibit nearly all characteristics of a Proof.

recolored, retoned. Descriptive of a coin's surface which has been artificially colored by use of heat, a chemical substance, or other agent, or which has had the toning accelerated to a short period of time, thus giving coloration or toning intended to be similar to natural toning acquired over a long period of time.

recut date, recut mintmark. Descriptive of a recut date, mintmark, or other feature in which the figure has been strengthened in the die by punching it again, thus creating a slight doubling in coins struck from these dies. Among 19th-century coins, recut dates and letters are common. "Repunched" is a preferable term, but "recut" is in common usage.

reeded edge. An edge which is characterized by a series of vertical ribs or bars, typical of the edge found on most United States silver and gold coins.

reflective. Descriptive of a coin's surface which has mirror-like characteristics to reflect the light, or, in the manner of a mirror, to allow other objects to be reflected in it.

relief. The portion of a coin design which is raised, including on most issues the stars, lettering, portrait, etc., as opposed to flat surface of a coin. Compare with incuse, the opposite effect.

repair, repaired. A repaired coin is one which has had damage, a defect, a hole, or some other problem corrected by engraving, burnishing, filling with solder, or some other action. Repairs to a coin must always be described.

restrike. A coin struck from official dies but later than the date indicated. Restriking has been a common practice at the various United States mints over the years, and even in recent times restriking has taken place (for example, 1776-1976 Bicentennial coins were struck for several years after 1976). Certain early United States coins were restruck at substantially later times by mint officials and others who traded or sold them at a profit.

Examples include certain half cents dated in the 1840s, 1856 Flying Eagle cents, etc.

reverse. The back or "tail" side of a coin, typically the side with an eagle or other non-human representation, as opposed to the obverse which typically bears a human portrait and date. Many exceptions exist, particularly among United States commemorative coins.

rim. The outer edge of a coin's surface, obverse or reverse, often raised in order to protect the surface of the coin from wear (but not always raised; for example, 1908-1929 quarter eagles and half eagles have flat rims).

Roman Finish Proof. A special finish given to Proof gold coins at the Philadelphia Mint, circa 1909-1910, and consisting of a satiny finish of a brighter hue than the Matte Proof or Sandblast Proof surfaces used contemporaneously. The Roman Finish Proof was one of several finishes experimented with during the second decade of the 20th century.

rubbing. The result of a coin having sliding contact with a hard surface, thus wearing away the mint lustre and showing evidence of friction.

rusted dies. Dies which have acquired rust during storage and as a result have areas showing pitting or etching. Coins struck from rusted dies, certain varieties of 1833 quarter dollars for example, show these pitted or rusted areas raised on the coin's surface. Evidence of a coin having been struck from rusted dies has no effect on the grade of a coin.

Sandblast Proof. Descriptive of a Proof finish given to gold coins of the Pratt and Saint-Gaudens types, created by impinging minute sand particles against the coin's surface after striking. At the time, this process was a popular one for the finish of medals. Sandblast Proofs, commonly called Matte Proofs (although other varieties of Matte Proofs exist, and Matte Proof Lincoln cents, for example, were not made by the sandblast process), have a dull, minutely porous finish.

Satin Finish Proof. A Proof finish, a cross between a Matte Proof and an Uncirculated or business strike surface, seen on certain varieties of Pratt and Saint-Gaudens gold coins. One of several Proof finishes experimented with during this time in mint history.

scratch. A groove or line placed on a coin by a sharp pointed object, after the coin was struck, and recessed in the surface of the coin. Under high magnification, a scratch will show displaced metal as a tiny raised area on one side or both sides of the scratch (as compared with adjustment marks, made on the planchet before striking, which do not show areas of displaced metal).

sealed holder. A plastic holder, popularly called a "slab," with transparent face and back, used for the storage of a coin, and sealed at the edges by use of heat, a chemical agent, or a sonic device, in an effort to encapsulate a coin so that its grade will remain "permanent." Often sealed holders have a piece of cardboard or other identification in the holder which states someone's opinion of the coin's grade. In practice, such holders occasionally come apart, or are split apart, and coins of other grades may be substituted, so it is recommended that no coins ever be bought in a sealed holder without verification that the coin matches the grade stated on the holder.

semiprooflike. Used as a single word, or hyphenated as semi-prooflike, not capitalized. An adjective describing a coin with a partially mirror-like surface; with fields or background consisting of a mixture of mint lustre and frost with some mirror-like characteristics.

Sheldon Scale. The numerical system of grading proposed by Dr. William H. Sheldon, a New York City psychiatrist, in 1949, and delineated in his book *Early American Cents*. Numbers from 1 through 70 were given to coins, the number 1 referring to Basal State, or a coin in Poor grade barely identifiable as to type, up to MS-70, or a perfect coin. The system was part of a market formula to determine the price of large cents of the 1793-1814 years. Later, others, notably the American Numismatic Association Board of Governors and various committees formed by it, expanded the system far beyond Dr. Sheldon's original ideas or intentions, thus creating the ANA grading system.

silver. A precious metal used to produce United States coins from 1794 through 1964, and occasionally later (for commemorative issues). In coinage, nine parts of silver are mixed with one part copper, the copper adding strength. The resultant alloy is known as coin silver, although numismatists simply refer to a coin as being made of silver.

slab. A slang term descriptive of a sonically sealed or chemically sealed plastic holder encapsulating a coin, and also containing a printed description of someone's opinion of that coin's grade. A coin which has been so encapsulated is designated as having been slabbed.

slider. A slang term referring to a coin which shows friction marks or evidence of sliding contact, a coin which is separated from the Uncirculated category by such evidences and which is therefore properly called About Uncirculated.

specimen, specimen striking. (1) Any individual coin can be referred to as a specimen of a coin; in other words, an example of a coin; a piece. (2) A specimen striking is a piece, either a business strike or a Proof coin, which has been specially prepared at the mint and handled with care, with the intention of presenting the coin or selling it to someone desiring it for a collection or for other non-circulating purposes. A specimen coin is one with a very attractive finish, showing evidence of careful striking. In Canada, the term specimen, capitalized as Specimen, is a synonym for a Proof coin.

split grade. The designation of separate grades for the obverse and reverse of the same coin. Thus, a coin which has an MS-63 obverse and an MS-65 reverse is graded MS-63/65, and is a split grade coin.

strike, striking. References to the actual coining process, although sometimes used as a noun. Thus, a coin designated as a sharp strike is a coin which has all the design details sharply struck. A flat strike or a weak strike is one which has the features lightly or indistinctly impressed.

sweated. A procedure by which a coin, especially a gold coin, is subjected to treatment by acid to remove some of the metal (which can later be recovered at a profit from the solution), in the process imparting a grainy or pebbly effect to the surface. This was employed by jewelers, bullion merchants, and others in the past to make an illegal profit from coins passing through their hands.

technical grade. The adjectival or numerical grade given to a coin, such as Very Fine (adjectival grade) or VF-30 (numerical grade). This technical grade consists of a description or numerical designation applied by a coin grader and does not describe other aspects determining a coin's value, such as sharpness of striking, centering on the planchet, surface quality, aesthetic appeal, etc. Thus, for example, a coin can have a technical grade of MS-65 but have the market value of an MS-60 or MS-63 coin, a fact often overlooked by persons concentrating on the technical aspects only.

toning, toned surface. Descriptive of coloration, patina, or tarnish (although tarnish is seldom used, for many view it as a negative term) which has been deposited on a coin, either over a long period of time (natural toning) or artificially by means of heat, chemicals, or some other process (artificial toning). Attractive natural toning can sharply increase the value of a coin.

typical. A term invented by Kenneth E. Bressett and used in the first and second editions of *Official ANA Grading Standards for United States Coins* to describe a low-level Uncirculated or Proof coin. Thus, a Typical Uncirculated coin was a minimum Uncirculated coin, or a Mint State-60 (MS-60) example, while a Typical Proof coin was a Proof-60 example. In the third edition of the book, released in 1987, the "typical" term was no longer employed.

Uncirculated. Descriptive of a business strike coin which has never been in circulation. Known as Mint State under the Sheldon Scale and the numerical grading system. On the adjectival system, Uncirculated coins can be described as Uncirculated, Choice Uncirculated, Gem Uncirculated, etc. In the numerical system, the American Numismatic Association employs all numbers from MS-60 to MS-70, a total of 11, for MS-60, MS-61, MS-62, etc.

undergrading. The opposite of overgrading, although undergrading is so seldom practiced that this very term will seem unfamiliar to most readers (a little humor here!).

verdigris. Grease, dirt, and other foreign elements adhering to the surface of a coin, in the spaces and recesses among letters, etc., but not chemically a part of a coin's surface. Verdigris is removable with soap and water or a solvent. The removal of such does not change the surface characteristics or coloration of a coin.

Very Fine. A grading term, capitalized, designating a coin which has had some wear, but which has all the lettering and other features distinctly readable. A detailed description of this and other grades are found elsewhere in the present text. In the Sheldon Scale and the ANA grading system Very Fine is designated as Very Fine-20, Very Fine-30 (this being Choice Very Fine according to the ANA), and the grade often used among copper specialists, but not by the ANA, Very Fine-35.

Very Good. A grading term, capitalized, describing a piece which has extensive wear but which has most letters and devices visible. In the Sheldon Scale and the ANA grading system, designated as Very Good-8, abbreviated as VG-8.

weak strike. Descriptive of a coin which has certain areas weakly or poorly defined because of incomplete striking during the minting process.

wear. The process by which a coin in circulation gradually loses metal through handling and contact with other surfaces. As metal is taken away, the coin becomes more and more worn.

whizzed, whizzing. A whizzed coin is one which has been treated with a wire brush or mechanical tool which imparts a series of microscopic grooves in the piece, falsely giving the appearance of mint frost or lustre. Whizzed coins were a numismatic threat in the 1960s and 1970s, until Virgil Hancock mounted a campaign against those engaging in the practice. Today, the practice is less prevalent, but still whizzed coins are occasionally seen. In a grading description, whizzing must be noted.

wire brushed, wire brushing. Descriptive of a coin which has had the surfaces treated with a wire brush, thus giving it a series of parallel minute grooves somewhat resembling mint lustre, but distinguishable under high magnification. Refer to whizzing above.

wire rim. A rim or border of a coin which has been formed into a thin wirelike projection, the result of excess metal being squeezed between the edge of the die and the restraining collar. Wire rims are seen on certain Proof coins, particularly those of the 19th century, and certain other coins struck carefully under slow pressure (such as certain varieties of the MCMVII High Relief $20 pieces).